WeightWatchers®

Meals to share or just for you

For One & Two

First published in Great Britain by Simon & Schuster UK Ltd, 2013
A CBS Company

Copyright © 2013, Weight Watchers International, Inc.
Simon & Schuster Illustrated Books, Simon & Schuster UK Ltd,
First Floor, 222 Gray's Inn Road, London WC1X 8HB

www.simonandschuster.co.uk

Simon & Schuster Australia, Sydney
Simon & Schuster India, New Delhi

Weight Watchers Publications: Jane Griffiths, Linda Palmer and Nina McKerlie.

Recipes written by: Sue Ashworth, Sue Beveridge, Tamsin Burnett-Hall,
Cas Clarke, Siân Davies, Roz Denny, Nicola Graimes, Becky Johnson,
Kim Morphew, Joy Skipper, Penny Stephens and Wendy Veale as well
as Weight Watchers Leaders and Members.

Photography by: Iain Bagwell, Steve Baxter, Steve Lee, Juliet Piddington
and William Shaw.
Project editor: Nicki Lampon.
Design and typesetting: Martin Lampon.

Colour reproduction by Dot Gradations Ltd, UK.
Printed and bound in China.

A CIP catalogue for this book is available from the British Library

ISBN 978-1-47111-085-6

1 2 3 4 5 6 7 8 9 10

Pictured on the title page: Beef en croûte p40.
Pictured on the Introduction: Almond glazed duck with asparagus p86, Fresh fig tart
p150, Spicy prawn open ravioli p102.

WeightWatchers®

Meals to share or just for you

For One & Two

SIMON &
SCHUSTER
ILLUSTRATED

London · New York · Sydney · Toronto · New Delhi

A CBS COMPANY

Weight Watchers **ProPoints** Weight Loss System is a simple way to lose weight. As part of the Weight Watchers **ProPoints** plan you'll enjoy eating delicious, healthy, filling foods that help to keep you feeling satisfied for longer and in control of your portions.

Ⓥ This symbol denotes a vegetarian recipe and assumes that, where relevant, free range eggs, vegetarian cheese, vegetarian virtually fat free fromage frais, vegetarian low fat crème fraîche and vegetarian low fat yogurts are used. Virtually fat free fromage frais, low fat crème fraîche and low fat yogurts may contain traces of gelatine so they are not always vegetarian. Please check the labels.

❄ This symbol denotes a dish that can be frozen. Unless otherwise stated, you can freeze the finished dish for up to 3 months. Defrost thoroughly and reheat until the dish is piping hot throughout.

Recipe notes

Egg size: Medium sized, unless otherwise stated.

Raw eggs: Only the freshest eggs should be used. Pregnant women, the elderly and children should avoid recipes with eggs that are not fully cooked or raw.

All fruits and vegetables: Medium sized, unless otherwise stated.

Stock: Stock cubes are used in recipes, unless otherwise stated. These should be prepared according to packet instructions.

Recipe timings: These are approximate and meant to be guidelines. Please note that the preparation time includes all the steps up to and following the main cooking time(s).

Microwaves: Timings and temperatures are for a standard 800 W microwave. If necessary, adjust your own microwave.

Low fat spread: Where a recipe states to use a low fat spread, a light spread with a fat content of no less than 38% should be used.

Low fat soft cheese: Where low fat soft cheese is specified in a recipe, this refers to soft cheese with a fat content of less than 5%.

Contents

Introduction

It's easy to feel uninspired when it comes to cooking for yourself or just for two. It may seem too much effort, or all your favourite recipes are for four people and hard to produce for smaller numbers. *For One & Two* is here to help, filled with the best recipes from Weight Watchers cookbooks just for yourself or to share.

From a filling soup to a classic casserole, a quick stir-fry to an amazing dessert, there are so many great ideas here to get you cooking. Treat yourself to an individual Chicken and Sweetcorn Pie or Samon en Croûte, followed by Flaked Rice Pudding or a Peach Brûlée, or share a Superquick Spinach and Cheese Lasagne or Beef Stroganoff for Two followed by Easy Chocolate Soufflés. So next time you are cooking for one or two, create something delicious, healthy and stunning with the help of these wonderful recipes.

About Weight Watchers

For more than 40 years Weight Watchers has been helping people around the world to lose weight using a long term sustainable approach. Weight Watchers successful weight loss system is based on four tried and trusted principles:

- Eating healthily
- Being more active
- Adjusting behaviour to help weight loss
- Getting support in weekly meetings

Our unique ***ProPoints*** system empowers you to manage your food plan and make wise recipe choices for a healthier, happier you.

To find out more about Weight Watchers and the ***ProPoints*** values for these recipes contact Customer Service on 0845 345 1500.

Storing and freezing

Many recipes in this book store well in the fridge, but make sure you use them up within a day or two. Some can also be frozen. If you are cooking for yourself, try making some of the recipes for two and storing the extra portions in the freezer. You can also double up the quantities in all of the recipes if you wish. This way you'll always have a fantastic selection of meals that you can pull out and reheat at the end of a busy day. However, it is important to make sure you know how to freeze safely.

- Wrap any food to be frozen in rigid containers or strong freezer bags. This is important to stop foods contaminating each other or getting freezer burn.
- Label the containers or bags with the contents and date – your freezer should have a star marking that tells you how long you can keep different types of frozen food.
- Never freeze warm food – always let it cool completely first.
- Never freeze food that has already been frozen and defrosted.
- Freeze food in portions, then you can take out as little or as much as you need each time.
- Defrost what you need in the fridge, making sure you put anything that might have juices, such as meat, on a covered plate or in a container.
- Fresh food, such as raw meat and fish, should be wrapped and frozen as soon as possible.
- Most fruit and vegetables can be frozen by open freezing. Lay them out on a tray, freeze until solid and then pack them into bags.
- Some vegetables, such as peas, broccoli and broad beans can be blanched first by cooking for 2 minutes in boiling water. Drain, refresh under cold water and then freeze once cold.

- Fresh herbs are great frozen – either seal leaves in bags or, for soft herbs such as basil and parsley, chop finely and add to ice cube trays with water. These are great for dropping into casseroles or soups straight from the freezer.

Some things cannot be frozen. Whole eggs do not freeze well, but yolks and whites can be frozen separately. Vegetables with a high water content, such as salad leaves, celery and cucumber, will not freeze. Fried foods will be soggy if frozen, and sauces such as mayonnaise will separate when thawed and should not be frozen.

Shopping hints and tips

Always buy the best ingredients you can afford. If you are going to cook healthy meals, it is worth investing in some quality ingredients that will really add flavour to your dishes. When buying meat, choose lean cuts of meat or lean mince, and if you are buying prepacked cooked sliced meat, buy it fresh from the deli counter.

When you're going around the supermarket it's tempting to pick up foods you like and put them in your trolley without thinking about how you will use them. So, a good plan is to decide what dishes you want to cook before you go shopping, check your store cupboard and make a list of what you need. You'll save time by not drifting aimlessly around the supermarket picking up what you fancy.

We've added a checklist here for some of the store cupboard ingredients used in this book. Just add fresh ingredients in your regular shop and you'll be ready to cook the wonderful recipes in *For One & Two*.

Store cupboard checklist

- [ ] almonds, flaked
- [ ] apricots, ready-to-eat
- [ ] artificial sweetener
- [ ] bay leaves
- [ ] caraway seeds
- [ ] cherries, canned
- [ ] chilli flakes
- [ ] chocolate, 70% cocoa solids
- [ ] cinnamon, ground
- [ ] coconut milk, reduced fat
- [ ] cooking spray, calorie controlled
- [ ] coriander, ground
- [ ] cornflour
- [ ] couscous, dried
- [ ] crab meat, canned
- [ ] cumin (seeds and ground)
- [ ] curry pastes
- [ ] fish sauce
- [ ] flour, plain white
- [ ] ginger, ground
- [ ] gravy granules

- [ ] haricot beans, canned
- [ ] herbs, dried
- [ ] honey, clear
- [ ] horseradish, grated in a jar
- [ ] kidney beans, canned
- [ ] lentils (canned green and dried Puy)
- [ ] mushroom ketchup
- [ ] mustard (Dijon and wholegrain)
- [ ] mustard seeds
- [ ] noodles (dried and straight-to-wok)
- [ ] nutmeg
- [ ] oil (olive, sesame and sunflower)
- [ ] pasta, dried
- [ ] peppercorns
- [ ] pesto, sun-dried tomato
- [ ] pine nut kernels
- [ ] pineapple rings, canned in natural juice
- [ ] pizza base mix
- [ ] polenta, dried

- [ ] rice, dried (brown and risotto)
- [ ] salt
- [ ] semolina, dried
- [ ] sesame seeds
- [ ] soy sauce
- [ ] sponge fingers
- [ ] stock cubes
- [ ] sugar (caster, demerara and light brown)
- [ ] sweet chilli sauce
- [ ] sweetcorn, canned
- [ ] Tabasco sauce
- [ ] teriyaki sauce
- [ ] tomato purée
- [ ] tomatoes, canned
- [ ] tomatoes, sun-dried
- [ ] turmeric
- [ ] vanilla extract
- [ ] vinegar (balsamic and white wine)
- [ ] wasabi paste
- [ ] Worcestershire sauce
- [ ] yellow bean sauce

Light bites

Chinese chicken noodle soup

Serves 1
268 calories
Takes 15 minutes

40 g (1½ oz) dried fine egg noodles, broken roughly
60 g (2 oz) baby corn, sliced thinly
300 ml (10 fl oz) chicken stock
1 teaspoon soy sauce
75 g (2¾ oz) cooked skinless chicken breast, sliced
2 spring onions, sliced

This Chinese-style favourite makes for a quick and very filling lunch or light supper.

1 Bring a pan of water to the boil, add the noodles and baby corn and cook for 3 minutes. Drain and rinse in cold water.

2 Pour the stock into the saucepan, add the soy sauce and bring to a simmer. Mix in the chicken, spring onions, cooked noodles and baby corn and heat through for 1–2 minutes until piping hot. Pour into a bowl and serve.

Variation... For a vegetarian version, see the recipe on page 16.

Mushroom noodle soup

Serves 1

181 calories

Takes 15 minutes

40 g (1½ oz) dried fine egg noodles, broken roughly

75 g (2¾ oz) button mushrooms, sliced

60 g (2 oz) baby corn, sliced thinly

300 ml (10 fl oz) vegetable stock

1 teaspoon soy sauce

2 spring onions, sliced

This fast and easy soup is a vegetarian version of the recipe on page 14.

1 Bring a pan of water to the boil, add the noodles, mushrooms and baby corn and cook for 3 minutes. Drain and rinse in cold water.

2 Pour the stock into the saucepan, add the soy sauce and bring to a simmer. Mix in the spring onions, cooked noodles, mushrooms and baby corn and cook for 1–2 minutes until piping hot. Pour into a bowl and serve.

Crunchy beef salad

Serves 2
437 calories per serving
Takes 20 minutes

This delicious Thai-inspired beef noodle dish also works well with leftover roast beef. Simply use 2 x 35 g (1½ oz) slices of roast beef per serving instead of the steak.

100 g (3½ oz) cucumber, de-seeded and grated coarsely

100 g (3½ oz) beansprouts

½ red pepper, de-seeded and sliced finely

2 tablespoons chopped fresh coriander

1–2 teaspoons wasabi paste

1 tablespoon sweet chilli sauce

juice of a lime

½ teaspoon fish sauce

2 teaspoons light soy sauce

2 x 125 g (4½ oz) fillet steaks, trimmed of visible fat

calorie controlled cooking spray

75 g (2¾ oz) dried rice noodles, broken in half

½ a kettleful of boiling water

15 g (½ oz) dry roasted peanuts, chopped, to garnish

1 In a large bowl, mix together the cucumber, beansprouts, pepper and coriander. Set aside. In a small jug, mix together the wasabi, chilli sauce, lime juice, fish sauce and soy sauce.

2 Heat a griddle pan or non stick frying pan until hot and spray the steaks with the cooking spray. Cook for 5–6 minutes, turning halfway, until cooked to your liking. Remove to a plate, cover loosely with foil and set aside for 5 minutes.

3 Meanwhile, soak the rice noodles in the boiling water and set aside for 5 minutes.

4 Drain and gently toss the noodles and dressing through the beansprout salad. Divide between two plates, slice the steak diagonally and place on top of the salads. Sprinkle over the peanuts and serve.

Chicken couscous salad

Serves 2
277 calories per serving
Takes 15 minutes + chilling
❄

150 ml (5 fl oz) hot chicken
    stock
100 g (3½ oz) dried couscous
grated zest and juice of
    ½ a lemon
2 tablespoons chopped fresh
    coriander
1 peach, stoned and chopped
8 cherry tomatoes, halved
4 spring onions, chopped
½ green or yellow pepper,
    de-seeded and sliced
175 g (6 oz) cooked skinless
    chicken breast, chopped
    into bite size pieces
salt and freshly ground black
    pepper

Couscous turns a regular salad into a filling option.

1 In a bowl, pour the hot chicken stock over the couscous
and stir in the lemon zest and juice and 1 tablespoon of the
coriander. Cover and leave to stand for 5 minutes.

2 Fluff up the couscous with a fork, transfer to a serving dish
and leave to cool completely.

3 When cool, stir in the fruit and vegetables and check the
seasoning. Stir in the chicken (or pop it on top of the salad) and
then scatter the remaining coriander over the top.

4 Chill until ready to use or transfer to a lunchbox and keep
cool.

Ⓥ **Variation...** For a vegetarian version, substitute Quorn
Deli Chicken Style Slices for the chicken and use vegetable
stock.

Shish kebabs with coriander relish

Serves 2

282 calories per serving

Takes 15 minutes to prepare,
10–12 minutes to cook

*The fresh tasting herby yogurt relish provides a perfect
accompaniment to these Indian-style lamb kebabs. Serve
with 60 g (2 oz) dried brown rice or bulgur wheat per
person, cooked according to the packet instructions.*

250 g (9 oz) lean minced lamb

½ small onion, grated

**1 heaped tablespoon chopped
fresh coriander**

½ teaspoon ground cumin

½ teaspoon ground coriander

**salt and freshly ground black
pepper**

For the relish

**15 g (½ oz) fresh coriander,
including the stalks,
chopped finely**

**1 heaped tablespoon chopped
fresh mint**

**½ small green chilli,
de-seeded and diced**

1 tablespoon lemon juice

**80 g (3 oz) low fat natural
yogurt**

1 Preheat the grill to medium and line the grill tray with foil.

2 Mix the minced lamb, onion, fresh coriander and spices
together well, adding plenty of seasoning.

3 Divide the mixture into 12 and shape into little sausages.
Thread on to four metal skewers. Grill for 10–12 minutes,
turning occasionally.

4 Meanwhile, mix the relish ingredients together, seasoning to
taste. If you have a mini processor you can blitz them together
to give a vibrantly green relish; otherwise, simply mix together
in a bowl. Serve alongside the cooked kebabs.

Florentine toast

Serves 1
285 calories
Takes 15 minutes

125 g (4½ oz) skinless smoked haddock fillet
1 bay leaf
1 egg
calorie controlled cooking spray
4 cherry tomatoes
a large handful of spinach leaves, washed
1 garlic clove, sliced
1 medium slice wholemeal bread
freshly ground black pepper

This makes a lovely brunch dish.

1 Place the haddock and bay leaf in a small, lidded, shallow pan and cover with water. Bring to the boil, cover and simmer gently for 5 minutes until the fish just flakes. Using a slotted spoon, remove the fish to a plate, cover and keep warm. Discard the bay leaf.

2 Bring the water that the haddock was in back to the boil and reduce to a simmer. Crack the egg into a small cup, stir the water creating a whirlpool effect and carefully add the egg to the water. Cook for 3–4 minutes, depending on how soft you like your egg yolk. Remove with a slotted spoon.

3 Meanwhile, spray a small non stick frying pan with the cooking spray and heat until hot. Add the tomatoes and fry for 2 minutes. Add the spinach and garlic with a tablespoon of water and continue cooking until the spinach has wilted. Remove from the heat.

4 Toast the bread until golden and then top with the spinach and tomatoes, haddock and poached egg. Season with black pepper and serve.

Tip... The bay leaf reduces the odour of the fish while cooking.

Scandinavian trout sandwich

Serves 2

435 calories per serving

Takes 10 minutes to prepare + cooling for the onion pickle, 3–5 minutes to cook

For the onion pickle

- 2 red onions, sliced finely, skins reserved
- 2 tablespoons white wine vinegar
- 1 tablespoon mustard seeds
- 2 teaspoons caster sugar
- ½ a kettleful of boiling water
- salt and freshly ground black pepper

For the trout

- 1 bay leaf
- 6 peppercorns
- 2 x 150 g (5½ oz) trout fillets
- 2 small pickled gherkins, sliced
- 2 tablespoons low fat mayonnaise
- 2 teaspoons wholegrain mustard
- a small bunch of fresh dill, chopped, plus a few whole sprigs to garnish
- 2 x 50 g (1¾ oz) slices rye bread

This appetising, pretty, open sandwich makes a refreshing lunch or light supper.

1 To make the onion pickle, place the sliced onion in an old jam jar with the vinegar, mustard seeds, sugar and seasoning. Pour in boiling water to cover and leave to cool before putting the lid on. Leave until completely cool, preferably overnight.

2 For the trout, bring a frying pan of water to the boil with the bay leaf, peppercorns and reserved onion skins. Add the trout fillets and poach for 3–5 minutes until just cooked through. Drain and set aside to cool.

3 Flake the trout fillets into a bowl and then add all the other ingredients for the trout except the bread and whole dill sprigs. Fold gently together.

4 To serve, spoon the trout on to pieces of rye bread and top with some of the onion pickle and the reserved dill sprigs.

◍ **Variation...** For a vegetarian alternative, use 100 g (3½ oz) of half fat Cheddar cheese slices instead of the trout.

Pastrami and sticky onion wraps

Serves 2
252 calories per serving
Takes 10 minutes

1 onion, peeled
½ teaspoon olive oil
2 soft flour tortillas
60 g (2 oz) low fat soft cheese
25 g (1 oz) wild rocket
4 slices pastrami
salt and freshly ground black
pepper

Fabulous for a lunch to take to work, wrap the filled tortillas in greaseproof paper or cling film to stop them from drying out.

1 Preheat the grill to medium.

2 Cut the onion into 10 or 12 wedges, slicing through the root so that the sections stay together. Place in a small non stick roasting tin, drizzle with the oil and 3 tablespoons of water, season and toss to coat.

3 Cook under the preheated grill for 6–8 minutes, turning once. The liquid will evaporate, softening the onions as they cook. Meanwhile, gently warm the tortillas to soften them, either by dry-frying for 15 seconds on each side, or by warming in the microwave for 15 seconds.

4 Spread each tortilla with half the soft cheese and then scatter on the rocket. Add the onions and two slices of pastrami each. Fold in one edge to form a base for the wrap and then roll up tightly.

Chicken, salami and courgette patties

Serves 1

305 calories

Takes 30 minutes

❄ (before cooking)

60 g (2 oz) cooked skinless chicken breast, cut into small pieces

2 x 6 g slices Milano salami, cut into small pieces

1 small courgette, grated coarsely

2 fresh basil leaves, shredded

2 tablespoons plain white flour

1 egg yolk

calorie controlled cooking spray

salt and freshly ground black pepper

Serve with 100 g (3½ oz) cooked new potatoes and a generous salad.

1 Preheat the oven to Gas Mark 6/200°C/fan oven 180°C and put a non stick baking tray in to heat. Mix together the chicken, salami, courgette, basil, flour and seasoning in a bowl until combined.

2 Stir in the egg yolk and, using wet hands, shape the mixture into three patties. Transfer to the preheated baking tray and spray with the cooking spray. Bake in the oven for 15–20 minutes until golden, turning halfway through the cooking time. Serve immediately.

Moules provençale

Serves 1
294 calories
Takes 10 minutes

1 teaspoon olive oil
1 small onion, chopped finely
1 celery stick, sliced
1 small courgette, diced
1 garlic clove, sliced
230 g can chopped tomatoes
   with herbs
500 g (1 lb 2 oz) fresh
   mussels, prepared (see Tip)
salt and freshly ground black
   pepper

Mussels in their shells are very easy and quick to cook, and because they take longer to eat they seem very filling. This tomato based sauce is full of the flavours of the Mediterranean, so make sure you've got a spoon ready to scoop up all the goodness. Serve with a 50 g (1¾ oz) crusty bread roll.

1 Heat the oil in a large, lidded, non stick saucepan, add the onion and cook for 2 minutes. Add the celery, courgette and garlic and cook for a further 2 minutes.

2 Add the tomatoes, mussels and 3 tablespoons of water and season. Toss the mussels around in the sauce and then cover the pan and cook for 5 minutes over a moderate heat, shaking the pan a couple of times until the mussels have opened. Discard any mussels that stay closed after cooking.

3 Tip into a deep warmed bowl to serve and have another bowl ready to put the empty shells in as you eat.

Tip... To prepare mussels, scrub off any dirt and remove any barnacles. Remove the beard, if any, that sticks out between the shells. Discard any mussels that are already open or have a cracked shell.

Cheese and spinach quesadilla

Serves 1

317 calories

Takes 10 minutes

1 soft flour tortilla

1 teaspoon Dijon or French mustard

40 g (1½ oz) half fat mature Cheddar cheese, grated

2 teaspoons onion chutney

1 tomato, sliced

a small handful of baby spinach, washed

This toasted sandwich, originally from Mexico, is delicious served with a simple salad and 1 tablespoon reduced fat coleslaw.

1 Put the tortilla on a board and spread the mustard all over it. Mix together the cheese and chutney in a small bowl. Spread the cheese mixture over one half of the tortilla and then top with the tomato slices and spinach. Fold the tortilla in half to make a semi-circle.

2 Heat a non stick frying pan or griddle pan until hot. Put the tortilla in the pan and cook for 1–2 minutes until slightly golden, holding it in place with a spatula (otherwise it will unfold).

3 Carefully turn over the tortilla using the spatula and cook for another 1–2 minutes until golden and the cheese has melted. Remove to a board, cut in half and serve immediately.

Variation... For a non-vegetarian version, try adding 30 g (1¼ oz) wafer thin chicken.

Minty lamb burgers

Serves 2
246 calories per serving
Takes 20 minutes + chilling
❄

225 g (8 oz) lean minced lamb
1 small onion, quartered
1 garlic clove
10 fresh mint leaves
60 g (2 oz) salsa
salt and freshly ground black
  pepper
a selection of salad
  vegetables, to serve

You can cook these under the grill or on a barbecue. They are perfect for a summer's day.

1 Put the lamb, onion, garlic and mint in a food processor with a little seasoning and blend until it comes together as a ball. (If you don't have a food processor, chop everything as finely as possible and then use your hands to squeeze it together.)

2 Using wet hands, shape the meat into four burgers. Place them on a plate and leave to chill in the fridge for at least an hour.

3 Preheat the grill to medium or ensure your barbecue is ready. Cook the burgers for 5 minutes on each side or until cooked through.

4 Serve the burgers topped with the salsa and with your choice of salad vegetables.

Tip... Like your burgers a bit spicy? Omit the mint and use 1 tablespoon chopped fresh coriander, ½ a small de-seeded chilli and 1 teaspoon ground cumin.

8oz lean Lamb 11 points

∴ 1 burge 6 points

Parsnip cakes with poached egg

Serves 1

292 calories

Take 5 minutes to prepare,
10 minutes to cook

calorie controlled cooking
spray
1 teaspoon vinegar (any type)
1 egg
salt and freshly ground black
pepper
a handful of fresh parsley,
chopped, to garnish
(optional)

For the parsnip cakes

150 g (5½ oz) parsnip, peeled
and grated coarsely
½ onion, grated coarsely
1 garlic clove, crushed
a few thyme sprigs, woody
stems removed, chopped
finely
1 small egg, beaten

A perfect brunch dish, this a real treat for days when you just have yourself to cook for.

1 Place all the ingredients for the parsnip cakes in a bowl, season and mix together.

2 Heat a large non stick frying pan and spray with the cooking spray. Place four spoonfuls of the parsnip mixture well apart in the pan and flatten into thin rounds with a fish slice or the back of a spoon. Fry on a low to medium heat for about 3–4 minutes until golden brown, then turn over and cook for another 4 minutes. Transfer the cakes to a plate and keep warm while you cook the rest of the mixture the same way.

3 To poach the egg, bring a pan of water to the boil and add the vinegar. Reduce the water to a simmer. Crack the egg into a small cup, stir the water creating a whirlpool effect and carefully add the egg to the water. Cook for 3–4 minutes, depending on how soft you like your egg yolk, and then fish out with a slotted spoon.

4 Serve the egg on a pile of parsnip cakes with a scattering of fresh parsley, if using.

Parsnip Raw 1 medium
2 points

Marvellous meat

Beef en croûte

Serves 2

425 calories per serving

Takes 25 minutes to prepare,
20 minutes to cook

❄

1 teaspoon sunflower oil

2 x 125 g (4½ oz) beef fillet
steaks, trimmed of visible fat

2 large open cup mushrooms

25 g (1 oz) dolcelatte cheese,
crumbled

15 g (½ oz) fresh white
breadcrumbs

4 x 45 g (1½ oz) sheets filo
pastry, measuring
50 x 24 cm (20 x 9½ inches)

15 g (½ oz) low fat spread,
melted

salt and freshly ground black
pepper

*This dish looks very impressive, so it is well worth the
effort for a special occasion.*

1 Heat the oil in a non stick frying pan and fry the steaks for
1 minute on each side to seal them. Remove the steaks from
the pan.

2 Remove the stalks from the mushrooms and set them aside.
Add the mushrooms to the pan, cup side down. Cook for
2 minutes until they begin to soften and then drain them on
kitchen towel.

3 Chop the mushroom stalks very finely and mix them with the
cheese, breadcrumbs and seasoning. Pack this mixture into the
cup of the mushrooms, pressing down well. Place a mushroom,
filled side down, on top of each steak.

4 Preheat the oven to Gas Mark 6/200°C/fan oven 180°C. Line
a baking tray with non stick baking parchment.

5 Brush each sheet of filo pastry with the melted low fat
spread and stack two sheets together, so you have two piles
of pastry. Wrap each mushroom topped steak in a double
layer of pastry and brush the surface with any remaining
melted spread.

6 Bake in the oven for 20 minutes until the pastry is crisp and
golden.

Lamb and lentil curry

Serves 2
277 calories per serving
Takes 30 minutes
❄

This warming and sustaining curry freezes well, so it is well worth making double the quantity and freezing half for future use. Serve with a Weight Watchers Plain Poppadom each.

calorie controlled cooking spray
1 large onion, sliced
160 g (5¾ oz) lean minced lamb
2 large garlic cloves, crushed
2 tablespoons tikka masala paste
300 ml (10 fl oz) vegetable stock
3 tablespoons canned chopped tomatoes
175 g (6 oz) baby spinach, washed
6 tablespoons canned green lentils, drained
salt and freshly ground black pepper
a handful of chopped fresh coriander, to garnish (optional)

1 Heat a large non stick saucepan and spray with the cooking spray. Add the onion and cook, stirring, for 3 minutes. Stir in the mince and cook for 2 minutes until browned.

2 Add the garlic to the pan and cook for another minute before stirring in the tikka masala paste, stock and tomatoes. Cook for 15 minutes, stirring occasionally, and then add the spinach and lentils. Season and cook for a final 5 minutes.

3 Serve garnished with the fresh coriander, if using.

Pepperoni pizza

Serves 2

310 calories per serving

Takes 25 minutes to prepare,
12–15 minutes to cook

❄ (sauce only)

½ x 144 g packet pizza base mix

For the topping

calorie controlled cooking spray

½ small onion, chopped finely

1 garlic clove, crushed

a generous pinch of dried chilli flakes

1 teaspoon dried oregano

200 g can chopped tomatoes

1 yellow pepper, de-seeded and quartered lengthways

30 g (1¼ oz) sliced pepperoni

50 g (1¾ oz) cherry tomatoes, halved

75 g (2¾ oz) mozzarella light, sliced

25 g (1 oz) rocket

salt and freshly ground black pepper

A classic favourite, this version is far healthier than shop-bought or take-away pizzas.

1 Spray a small non stick saucepan with the cooking spray and place over a medium heat. Add the onion and garlic and cook for 5 minutes until softened, adding a little water if necessary to prevent the mixture from sticking. Add the chilli flakes, oregano and chopped tomatoes. Bring to the boil and simmer for about 20 minutes until thickened.

2 Meanwhile, make up the pizza dough according to the packet instructions. Set aside in a bowl covered with a clean tea towel until needed.

3 Preheat the grill to high. Put the pepper quarters on a baking tray, spray with the cooking spray and cook under the grill for about 5–7 minutes, turning once, until the skins have blackened. Remove from the grill, place in a bowl and leave to cool. When cool, peel off the skins and slice the peppers lengthways into thick strips.

4 Preheat the oven to Gas Mark 7/220°C/fan oven 200°C. Divide the dough in half and shape each piece into a 20 cm (8 inch) circle. Spray a non stick baking tray with the cooking spray and place the pizzas on it. Divide the tomato sauce between the bases and top with the pepperoni, pepper, tomatoes and mozzarella. Season.

5 Bake for 12–15 minutes until the dough is golden and the cheese is bubbling. Remove from the oven and transfer each pizza to a serving plate. Top each with half of the rocket and serve immediately.

Quick curried pork

Serves 1
188 calories
Takes 15 minutes

**calorie controlled cooking
    spray**
1 garlic clove, crushed
**1 teaspoon Thai red curry
    paste**
**100 g (3½ oz) lean pork steak,
    trimmed of visible fat and
    sliced finely**
**2.5 cm (1 inch) fresh root
    ginger, chopped finely**
2 tablespoons vegetable stock
1 tablespoon soy sauce
**2 tablespoons reduced fat
    coconut milk**
½ teaspoon turmeric
juice of ½ a lemon
**4 pickled garlic cloves,
    chopped finely**

*A very quick curry for one. It is delicious served with
60 g (2 oz) dried egg noodles, cooked according to the
packet instructions.*

1 Heat a large non stick frying pan, spray with the cooking
spray and stir-fry the garlic until golden brown. Add the curry
paste and stir in.

2 Add the pork and stir-fry for another 2 minutes until the
pork is browned. Add the remaining ingredients in turn, stirring
constantly for a minute or so until heated through.

Teriyaki beef udon

Serves 1
453 calories
Takes 15 minutes

calorie controlled cooking spray
125 g (4½ oz) lean rump steak, trimmed of visible fat
½ red onion, sliced
50 g (1¾ oz) sugar snap peas, halved lengthways
75 g (2¾ oz) mushrooms, sliced
2 tablespoons teriyaki sauce
1 teaspoon cornflour
150 g packet straight-to-wok udon noodles

This Japanese dish uses thick udon noodles, a classic Japanese ingredient.

1 Heat a non stick frying pan until hot and spray with the cooking spray. Fry the steak for 2½–3 minutes on each side over a high heat and then transfer to a warm plate and leave to rest.

2 Add the onion to the pan and fry for 1 minute and then add the sugar snap peas and mushrooms plus 1 tablespoon of water. Stir-fry for 2 minutes. Mix the teriyaki sauce with the cornflour and 4 tablespoons of cold water, add to the frying pan and cook for 1 minute.

3 Mix the udon noodles into the sauce and vegetables. Cook for 1–2 minutes until heated through. Slice the steak thinly and serve on top of the noodles.

Variation... See the recipe on page 140 for a wonderful vegetarian version.

Szechuan pork

Serves 1
690 calories
Takes 30 minutes

2 teaspoons Szechuan
   peppercorns
¼ teaspoon flaked sea salt
150 g (5½ oz) pork fillet,
   trimmed of visible fat
calorie controlled cooking
   spray
60 g (2 oz) dried wide rice
   noodles
1 pak choi, halved
2 teaspoons shredded fresh
   root ginger
2 teaspoons teriyaki sauce,
   to serve

Tender pieces of pork coated in a peppery spice go
beautifully with noodles and pak choi.

1 Place the peppercorns in a dry frying pan over a medium
heat and heat until toasted and fragrant. Place in a pestle and
mortar with the salt and crush together. Sprinkle the pork with
the salt and pepper mixture, patting it into the meat.

2 Spray a frying pan with the cooking spray and cook the pork
for 4–5 minutes on each side, or until cooked to your liking.
Allow the pork to stand in the pan, off the heat, for 5 minutes.

3 Meanwhile, bring a pan of water to the boil, add the noodles
and cook for 4 minutes or according to the packet instructions.
Drain.

4 Place the pak choi in a steamer (if you don't have a steamer
you can use a metal colander over a pan), sprinkle with the
ginger and cook for 3–5 minutes, until it is tender.

5 Serve the pork, sliced, on top of the pak choi and wide rice
noodles. Drizzle with the teriyaki sauce.

Lamb's liver with balsamic vinegar, sage and apple

Serves 2
270 calories per serving
Takes 25 minutes

350 g (12 oz) swede, peeled and diced

2 spring onions, chopped

2 tablespoons skimmed milk

1 teaspoon olive oil

200 g (7 oz) lamb's liver, cut into strips

1 small red apple, cored and cut into 8 wedges

150 ml (5 fl oz) unsweetened apple juice

1 tablespoon balsamic vinegar

3 fresh sage leaves, torn, or ½ teaspoon dried sage

salt and freshly ground black pepper

This modern twist on an old favourite is served on a bed of crushed swede.

1 Bring a pan of water to the boil, add the swede and cook for 10 minutes. Drain, add the spring onions and milk, cover and keep warm on the hob.

2 Heat a non stick frying pan and add the oil and liver. Stir-fry for 1 minute. Add the apple wedges and stir-fry for a further 1 minute. Stir in the apple juice, balsamic vinegar and sage and cook over a high heat for 3–5 minutes until the liquid has nearly all evaporated.

3 Mash the swede and season well. Spoon on to plates and top with the liver and any remaining juices.

Tip... Balsamic vinegar has a uniquely intense flavour and is comparable to a fine bottle of wine, sometimes in price too. However it's well worth investing in this highly valued product from Modena, Italy, so that you can enjoy the intensity of just a few drops in dressings and sauces.

Variation... For a treat, you could try calf's liver in this recipe. Pork or turkey strips work well too.

Roast pork chops with apple stuffing

Serves 2

410 calories per serving

Takes 15 minutes to prepare, 40 minutes to cook

calorie controlled cooking spray

1 large eating apple, cored and grated

2 shallots, chopped finely

2 tablespoons grated horseradish from a jar

1 tablespoon Dijon mustard

4 x 100 g (3½ oz) pork chops, trimmed of visible fat

6 tablespoons balsamic vinegar

salt and freshly ground black pepper

This recipe is great served with braised red cabbage.

1 Preheat the oven to Gas Mark 4/180°C/fan oven 160°C and heat a large non stick frying pan. Spray with the cooking spray and stir-fry the apple and shallots with a couple of tablespoons of water until softened.

2 Remove from the heat and stir in the horseradish and mustard. With a small knife make a pocket in each pork chop by cutting a 4 cm (1½ inch) slit in the side of the meat opposite the bone. Move the knife back and forth inside the meat to make a pocket.

3 Push the apple stuffing into the pocket until the chops are plump and rounded. Lay them on a foil-lined baking tray.

4 Season the chops and drizzle over the balsamic vinegar. Roast for about 30 minutes or until the chops and stuffing are cooked through.

Steak and ale pie

Just because you are cooking for one doesn't mean you can't have a delicious pie. This is the perfect portion size.

calorie controlled cooking spray

1 small onion, chopped finely

1 carrot, peeled and chopped finely

1 celery stick, chopped finely

1 fresh sage sprig, chopped (optional)

100 ml (3½ fl oz) chicken stock

100 g (3½ oz) mushrooms

75 g (2¾ oz) lean sirloin steak, trimmed of visible fat and cubed

1 teaspoon plain white flour

2 tablespoons ale

50 g (1¾ oz) ready-to-roll puff pastry

1 teaspoon skimmed milk, to glaze

salt and freshly ground black pepper

1 Heat a lidded non stick saucepan and spray with the cooking spray. Fry the onion, carrot, celery and sage, if using, for 5 minutes or until softened, adding a little stock if necessary to prevent them from sticking.

2 Add the mushrooms, season and stir-fry for a further 2 minutes. Remove all the vegetables to a plate.

3 Season the steak, spray the pan again and fry the meat until browned all over. Sprinkle with the flour, return the vegetables to the pan and stir them all together.

4 Pour over the remaining stock and the ale and bring to the boil. Reduce the heat, cover and simmer for 30 minutes on a low heat.

5 Meanwhile, roll out the puff pastry to fit an individual pie dish. Preheat the oven to Gas Mark 4/180°C/fan oven 160°C.

6 Spoon the cooked filling into the pie dish and lay the pastry on top, pressing down at the edges. Brush with the skimmed milk and cut a slit in the middle. Bake for 20–25 minutes or until golden.

Steak fajita

Serves 1

273 calories

Takes 10 minutes to prepare
+ 1 hour marinating,
10 minutes to cook

**50 g (1¾ oz) good quality
steak, trimmed of visible fat
and cut into thin strips**

juice of ½ a lime

1 small garlic clove, crushed

½ teaspoon olive oil

**½ green or red pepper,
de-seeded and cut into
strips**

1 mushroom, sliced

1 small onion, sliced

1 tomato, sliced

1 soft flour tortilla

**salt and freshly ground black
pepper**

*Steak and vegetables all wrapped up in a beautiful soft
flour tortilla. Delicious.*

1 Put the steak in a bowl with the lime juice, garlic and oil.
Cover and marinate for about 1 hour in the fridge.

2 Remove the steak from the marinade with a slotted spoon
and place it in a hot wok or large non stick frying pan. Stir-fry
for 1–2 minutes or until cooked to taste, then remove it and set
to one side. Add the vegetables to the pan with the remaining
marinade juices and stir-fry for 2–3 minutes.

3 Meanwhile, warm the tortilla by microwaving on high for
10–15 seconds, or heat in an oven according to the packet
instructions.

4 Return the steak to the pan with the vegetables, stir well
and season. Wrap the stir-fry in the warmed tortilla and serve
immediately.

Lamb steak provençale

Serves 1

315 calories

Takes 10 minutes to prepare,
20 minutes to cook

This wonderful fresh tomato and courgette sauce complements lamb perfectly, drawing out its delicate flavours. This is delicious served with a small portion of chips.

2 tomatoes, skinned and chopped

1 large garlic clove, crushed

2 spring onions, chopped

1 courgette, chopped

3 tablespoons dry white wine

1 fresh basil sprig, chopped, or ½ teaspoon dried basil

125 g (4½ oz) lean lamb steak, trimmed of visible fat

salt and freshly ground black pepper

1 Place the tomatoes in a lidded saucepan with the garlic, spring onions, courgette, wine and seasoning. If you are using dried basil, add it at this stage. Cook the mixture until it sizzles. Reduce the heat, cover and simmer gently for 10 minutes or until the vegetables have softened. If you are using fresh basil, mix it in at this stage.

2 Meanwhile, preheat the grill to medium high. Season the lamb steak and grill it for about 5 minutes on each side. Alternatively, you can cook it on a non stick griddle pan. If you like the lamb slightly pink, cook it until it feels lightly springy, or, if you like it well done, cook it until the meat is firm.

3 Spoon the sauce over the lamb to serve.

Variations... Try this recipe using a beef, pork or turkey steak – they will work equally well.

If you don't want to use wine you can substitute water.

Use this sauce for pasta. Make a double quantity and freeze in two single portions.

Gammon steak and pineapple noodles

Serves 2

457 calories per serving

Takes 15 minutes to prepare,
20 minutes to cook

100 g (3½ oz) dried rice noodles

a kettleful of boiling water

2 x 150 g (5½ oz) lean gammon steaks, trimmed of visible fat

1 small can pineapple rings in natural juice, drained (keep the juice and chop all but two of the rings)

calorie controlled cooking spray

1 garlic clove, sliced finely

200 g (7 oz) Savoy cabbage, shredded finely

1 tablespoon soy sauce

½ teaspoon dried chilli flakes

Gammon and pineapple is a classic combination, updated here by serving with noodles.

1 Place the rice noodles in a bowl and cover with boiling water. Leave to soak for 10 minutes or according to the packet instructions and then drain.

2 Preheat the grill to medium and place the gammon steaks side by side on the grill pan. Grill for 5–6 minutes.

3 Turn the steaks over and top each one with a pineapple ring and a teaspoon of pineapple juice. Grill for another 5 minutes, until the pineapple is golden around the edges.

4 Meanwhile, spray a large non stick frying pan or wok with the cooking spray and stir-fry the garlic for a few seconds. Add the cabbage, soy sauce, chilli flakes, pineapple pieces and juice.

5 With some scissors, cut the cooked rice noodles in half and then stir them into the stir-fried vegetables. Serve with the hot gammon and pineapple.

Ⓥ **Variation...** For a vegetarian version, see the recipe on page 131.

Beef stroganoff for two

Serves 2
225 calories per serving
Takes 25 minutes

Great for a romantic dinner. Serve this rich stew with plain boiled potatoes and a peppery watercress or rocket and tomato salad, drizzled with balsamic vinegar.

calorie controlled cooking spray
2 shallots, chopped
2 garlic cloves, sliced finely
2 x 150 g (5½ oz) rump or entrecôte steaks, 2.5 cm (1 inch) thick, trimmed of visible fat and sliced thinly
200 g (7 oz) chestnut mushrooms, sliced
100 ml (3½ fl oz) vegetable or meat stock
4 tablespoons virtually fat free plain fromage frais
salt and freshly ground black pepper

1 Heat a large non stick frying pan and spray with the cooking spray. Stir-fry the shallots and garlic for 5 minutes or until softened, adding a little water if necessary to prevent them from sticking.

2 Add the steak and mushrooms and season. Stir-fry on a high heat for 2–3 minutes, until the meat is browned all over.

3 With the heat still turned up high, quickly add the stock and bubble for a few seconds, scraping up any juices stuck to the bottom of the pan with a wooden spatula. Turn the heat off, allow to cool for a minute, stir in the fromage frais and serve.

French ham and bean casserole

Serves 1
327 calories
Takes 25 minutes

calorie controlled cooking spray
1 small onion, chopped finely
1 garlic clove, crushed
200 g (7 oz) canned chopped tomatoes
1 teaspoon tomato purée
2 fresh thyme sprigs, woody stems removed and leaves chopped
½ teaspoon dried oregano or Mediterranean herbs
1 celery stick, sliced finely
1 bay leaf
50 g (1¾ oz) thickly sliced lean ham, cubed
200 g (7 oz) canned haricot beans, drained and rinsed
a small bunch of fresh parsley, chopped
salt and freshly ground black pepper

This is a quick and satisfying stew for a cold night. Serve with spinach and mashed potatoes.

1 Spray a non stick frying pan with the cooking spray and fry the onion and garlic for 3 minutes, until softened, adding a tablespoon of water if necessary to prevent them from sticking.

2 Add the tomatoes, tomato purée, thyme, oregano or Mediterranean herbs, celery and bay leaf and bring to the boil. Season and simmer for 5 minutes until thick.

3 Add the ham and beans and simmer for a further 5 minutes. Stir through the parsley and serve.

Sausages in mushroom and onion gravy with parsley mash

Serves 2
295 calories per serving
Takes 35 minutes

350 g (12 oz) potatoes, peeled and quartered

175 g (6 oz) reduced fat pork and beef sausages

4 rounded teaspoons instant gravy granules

300 ml (10 fl oz) boiling water

1 onion, chopped

1 tablespoon medium sherry

50 g (1¾ oz) button mushrooms, halved

1 teaspoon mushroom ketchup or Worcestershire sauce

1 teaspoon dried Italian herbs

3 tablespoons skimmed milk

1 tablespoon chopped fresh parsley

salt and freshly ground black pepper

A plateful of sausages and mash – the ultimate comfort food.

1 Bring a pan of water to the boil, add the potatoes and cook for about 20 minutes, until tender.

2 Meanwhile, cook the sausages over a medium heat in a large non stick frying pan. Turn them often until they are well browned.

3 To make the gravy, mix the gravy granules with the boiling water.

4 Add the onion to the frying pan. Cook for 2–3 minutes and then add the gravy, sherry, mushrooms, mushroom ketchup or Worcestershire sauce and Italian herbs. Heat and simmer gently for 5 minutes. Season to taste.

5 Drain the potatoes and mash well. Add the milk and parsley. Season and beat vigorously with a wooden spoon to make the potatoes light and fluffy.

6 Reheat the mash over a low heat, stirring constantly to prevent it from sticking. Serve with the sausages and gravy.

Variations... For a delicious change, make the mash with 150 g (5½ oz) peeled chopped potato and 150 g (5½ oz) peeled chopped swede or butternut squash – just cook the two vegetables together.

Ⓥ For a vegetarian version, use vegetarian sausages and vegetarian gravy granules, and make sure you use mushroom ketchup rather than Worcestershire sauce.

Perfect poultry

Duck à l'orange

Serves 2
167 calories per serving
Takes 30 minutes

**calorie controlled cooking
  spray**
**2 x 100 g (3½ oz) skinless
  boneless duck breasts**
1 orange
200 ml (7 fl oz) chicken stock
**110 g (4 oz) carrots, peeled
  and cut into julienne sticks
  (see Tip)**

*Duck and orange is a classic combination and this quick
recipe would make an excellent special dinner for two.
Serve with steamed Savoy cabbage.*

1 Lightly spray a non stick frying pan with the cooking
spray and heat until hot. Add the duck breasts and cook for
3–4 minutes, turning until browned all over.

2 Remove the zest from the orange using a zester or grater
and then remove the skin with a sharp knife and segment the
orange, collecting any juice. Add the orange zest, segments
and any juice to the pan with the stock. Simmer for 10 minutes
until the duck is just tender.

3 Add the carrots and cook for a further 5 minutes.

Tip... To make julienne carrots, use a vegetable peeler to
cut thin ribbons along the length of the carrot and then cut
these into thin narrow strips. Alternatively, cut into small
thin sticks.

One pot rosemary chicken pasta

Serves 1

363 calories

Takes 10 minutes to prepare,
15 minutes to cook

calorie controlled cooking spray

125 g (4½ oz) skinless boneless chicken breast, diced

½ onion, chopped

1 small courgette, diced

1 garlic clove, crushed

210 g can chopped tomatoes

½ tablespoon chopped fresh rosemary or ½ teaspoon dried rosemary

40 g (1½ oz) dried penne

150 ml (5 fl oz) boiling water

salt and freshly ground black pepper

This speedy casserole is a complete meal with hardly any washing up.

1 Heat a lidded non stick saucepan until hot and spray with the cooking spray. Brown the chicken and onion for 2 minutes. Add the courgette and garlic and cook for 2 minutes more.

2 Add the tomatoes, rosemary, pasta and boiling water to the pan and season to taste. Bring to the boil and cook, partially covered, for 15 minutes or until the pasta is tender.

Ⓥ **Variation...** Try replacing the chicken with 125 g (4½ oz) Quorn Chicken Style Pieces for a vegetarian version of this recipe.

Chicken and sweetcorn pie

Serves 1

425 calories

Takes 25 minutes

❄ (before grilling)

200 g (7 oz) potatoes, peeled and diced

½ chicken stock cube, crumbled

calorie controlled cooking spray

125 g (4½ oz) skinless chicken breast fillet, diced

150 g (5½ oz) leeks, sliced

60 g (2 oz) frozen sweetcorn

40 g (1½ oz) low fat soft cheese

salt and freshly ground black pepper

This is ideal comfort food for one, but the recipe can easily be multiplied to make a family size pie.

1 Bring a lidded pan of water to the boil, add the potatoes and stock cube, cover and cook for 10–12 minutes until tender. Drain, reserving the stock, and then mash the potatoes with 2 tablespoons of the stock. Season.

2 Meanwhile, spray a lidded non stick saucepan with the cooking spray and stir-fry the chicken for 3 minutes until browned.

3 Stir in the leeks and 4 tablespoons of stock and season. Cover the pan and cook for 5 minutes. Add the sweetcorn and cook for 2 minutes more. Preheat the grill to high.

4 Stir the soft cheese into the chicken mixture to make a sauce, check the seasoning and then tip into a small flameproof baking dish. Spread the mashed potato on top, spray with the cooking spray and grill for 5 minutes to brown the top.

Spaghetti meatballs for two

Serves 2

286 calories per serving

Takes 20 minutes to prepare,
25 minutes to cook

❄ (sauce only)

calorie controlled cooking
spray
150 g (5½ oz) dried spaghetti
salt and freshly ground black
pepper

For the meatballs
200 g (7 oz) minced turkey
1 garlic clove, crushed
1 small onion, diced finely
1 carrot, peeled and grated
1 small egg white
1 teaspoon Worcestershire
sauce or soy sauce
a bunch of fresh basil,
chopped, reserving some for
garnish

For the sauce
1 small onion, chopped finely
1 garlic clove, crushed
400 g can chopped tomatoes
2 teaspoons soy sauce

A tasty classic that is easy but good enough for a special dinner too.

1 Mix all the meatball ingredients together in a bowl, season and roll small amounts into balls. Gently brown in a non stick frying pan sprayed with the cooking spray and then remove to a plate.

2 For the sauce, spray the pan again, stir-fry the onion and garlic until softened and then add the tomatoes and soy sauce. Simmer for 10 minutes, season and then add the meatballs.

3 Simmer for a further 15 minutes or until the meatballs are cooked through and the sauce is thick. Turn gently every now and then to ensure the meatballs cook evenly and don't stick.

4 Meanwhile, bring a pan of water to the boil, add the pasta and cook according to the packet instructions. Drain.

5 To serve, pile the spaghetti on to warmed plates and spoon the meatballs and sauce on top. Garnish with fresh basil.

Baked lemon turkey rolls

Serves 1

280 calories

Takes 10 minutes to prepare,
20 minutes to cook

2 x 75 g (2¾ oz) thin skinless turkey breast steaks

50 g (1¾ oz) cottage cheese with onion and chives

2 thin slices prosciutto

150 ml (5 fl oz) chicken or vegetable stock

1 tablespoon white wine

½ lemon, sliced into wedges

4 garlic cloves, unpeeled

4 cherry tomatoes, halved

150 g (5½ oz) dried tagliatelle

salt and freshly ground black pepper

a handful of fresh basil or parsley, chopped, to garnish (optional)

These stuffed rolls look really professional but are very easy to prepare.

1 Preheat the oven to Gas Mark 4/180°C/fan oven 160°C. Place a piece of cling film on the work surface and put the turkey steaks on top. Cover them with another piece of cling film and bash gently with a rolling pin to make the steaks bigger and thinner.

2 Remove the top sheet of cling film and spread the cottage cheese on the steaks. Season.

3 Roll up the turkey steaks and then roll each in a piece of prosciutto. Place the rolls in a small ovenproof dish.

4 Pour the stock and wine over the steaks and arrange the lemon wedges, whole garlic cloves and cherry tomatoes around them. Bake for 20 minutes.

5 Meanwhile, bring a pan of water to the boil, add the pasta and cook according to the packet instructions. Drain.

6 Remove the dish from the oven. Mash the baked garlic and lemon with a fork, removing the papery garlic skins and lemon rind. Serve the turkey rolls on top of the tagliatelle and spoon over the juices. Scatter with the basil or parsley, if using, and serve.

Malaysian chicken

Serves 1

211 calories

Takes 25 minutes

Tantalise the taste buds with this deliciously different twist on chicken. Serve with 60 g (2 oz) dried basmati rice, cooked according to the packet instructions, and a heap of steamed broccoli.

calorie controlled cooking spray

1 small onion, sliced

½ red chilli, de-seeded and chopped finely

150 g (5½ oz) skinless boneless chicken breast, diced

1 teaspoon light brown soft sugar

2 teaspoons soy sauce

4 tablespoons chicken stock or water

1 teaspoon rice vinegar or lime juice

1 Spray a lidded non stick saucepan with the cooking spray and fry the onion and chilli for 2 minutes.

2 Add the chicken and stir-fry for 1 minute over a high heat. Sprinkle in the sugar and cook for 1 minute more until caramelised.

3 Mix the soy sauce, stock and rice vinegar or lime juice together. Pour over the chicken, cover the pan and simmer gently for 10 minutes.

4 Remove the lid, increase the heat and bubble for 2 minutes until slightly reduced, tossing the chicken in the sauce to glaze.

Chicken and mushroom risotto

Serves 2
395 calories per serving
Takes 35 minutes
❄

1 teaspoon olive oil

125 g (4½ oz) skinless boneless chicken breast, sliced into thin strips

2 shallots, chopped finely

1 garlic clove, crushed

150 g (5½ oz) mushrooms, sliced

150 g (5½ oz) dried risotto rice

600 ml (20 fl oz) chicken stock

1 teaspoon chopped fresh tarragon

salt and freshly ground black pepper

Use proper risotto rice for this to get the right result.

1 Heat the olive oil in a large non stick frying pan and stir-fry the chicken for 2–3 minutes to seal it on all sides. Add the shallots, garlic and mushrooms to the pan and cook for a further 2 minutes.

2 Add the rice and then stir in a little stock. Once this has been absorbed, stir in a little more. Keep doing this until all the stock is used up, this will take about 20 minutes.

3 Add the tarragon and season to taste. Serve at once.

Tips... Risotto is really at its best as soon as it is made; if it is left and reheated, it becomes stodgy. Ideally it should have a creamy almost sloppy consistency – if you prefer it a little drier, just cook the rice for a few more minutes.

You can use cooked, leftover chicken for this recipe, too. You won't need to stir-fry it first though.

Cider and mustard chicken

Serves 1
285 calories
Takes 20 minutes

**calorie controlled cooking
   spray**
**125 g (4½ oz) skinless
   boneless chicken breast**
1 small onion, sliced
1 garlic clove, crushed
150 ml (5 fl oz) medium cider
1 teaspoon cornflour
**1 teaspoon wholegrain
   mustard**
15 g (½ oz) low fat soft cheese

*This is delicious with 60 g (2 oz) dried brown rice, cooked
according to the packet instructions. Add 50 g (1¾ oz)
chopped green beans for the final 3 minutes of cooking
time.*

1 Heat a small, lidded, non stick frying pan until hot and
spray with the cooking spray. Place the chicken in the pan
and scatter the onion around the chicken. Fry the chicken for
2 minutes on each side, stirring the onions occasionally. Add
the garlic and cook for 1 minute more.

2 Pour the cider into the pan and bubble rapidly for 2 minutes
until slightly reduced. Blend the cornflour with a little cold
water and add to the cider, followed by the mustard, stirring
until thickened.

3 Cover the pan and simmer for 8 minutes, until the chicken is
cooked. Stir the soft cheese into the sauce just before serving
to give a creamy finish.

⊙ Variation... Why not try a vegetarian version of this
recipe, using 2 Quorn Fillets, cooked from frozen, instead
of the chicken breast.

Spicy turkey pizza

Serves 2
335 calories per serving
Takes 35 minutes
❄ (topping only)

**calorie controlled cooking
   spray**
**23 cm (9 inch) ready-made
   thin and crispy pizza base**

For the topping

1 small onion, chopped finely
1 garlic clove, crushed
140 g (5 oz) minced turkey
2 teaspoons dried mixed herbs
210 g can chopped tomatoes
2 tomatoes, sliced
**1 red chilli, de-seeded and
   diced**
**salt and freshly ground black
   pepper**

*Make the topping in advance and this pizza is ideal for a
last minute meal.*

1 Preheat the oven to Gas Mark 7/220°C/fan oven 200°C.
Spray a non stick baking tray with the cooking spray.

2 To make the topping, spray a non stick saucepan with the
cooking spray and heat until sizzling. Add the onion and garlic
and stir-fry for 5 minutes until softened. Add the mince and
cook for 5 minutes over a medium heat until brown. Add the
herbs and chopped tomatoes, reduce the heat and simmer for
10 minutes. Season.

3 Place the pizza base on the baking tray and spread the
topping over it. Top with the tomato slices and sprinkle with
the chilli. Bake for 8–10 minutes until the base is golden. Cut
in half and serve.

Tip... The topping needs to be quite thick, so if it is too
runny, cook it for a further 5 minutes.

Variation... Most supermarkets now stock minced turkey,
but as an alternative you can use 140 g (5 oz) (about two)
chopped turkey steaks.

Creamy turkey crêpes

Serves 2
530 calories per serving
Takes 20 minutes

This recipe takes advantage of the ready-made crêpes that you can buy from supermarkets. The filling is quick, easy and tasty.

4 ready-made crêpes

calorie controlled cooking spray

200 g (7 oz) skinless turkey breast fillets, sliced into thin strips

2 tablespoons soy sauce

1 red pepper, de-seeded and sliced finely

2 small courgettes, sliced into thin strips

100 ml (3½ fl oz) vegetable stock

100 g (3½ oz) low fat soft cheese

salt and freshly ground black pepper

1 Wrap the crêpes in foil and place in a warm oven to heat through.

2 Spray a large non stick frying pan with the cooking spray. Stir-fry the turkey strips for 5 minutes, until nearly cooked through and golden.

3 Add the soy sauce, pepper and courgettes. Stir-fry for another 2 minutes or until the vegetables begin to soften. Stir in the stock and soft cheese.

4 Check the seasoning and divide the mixture between the warmed crêpes. Roll them up and serve.

Almond glazed duck with asparagus

Serves 2
308 calories per serving
Takes 20 minutes

300 g (10½ oz) asparagus
  spears
calorie controlled cooking
  spray
2 x 125 g (4½ oz) skinless
  duck breast fillets
2 tablespoons soy sauce
4 rounded teaspoons clear
  honey
15 g (½ oz) flaked almonds
½ red chilli, de-seeded and
  diced

*A lovely recipe for a special dinner for two. Serve with
60 g (2 oz) dried wild or jasmine rice per person, cooked
according to the packet instructions.*

1 Preheat the oven to Gas Mark 6/200°C/fan oven 180°C.
Place the asparagus in a shallow roasting tin, spray with the
cooking spray and drizzle with 2 tablespoons of water. Roast in
the oven for 8 minutes.

2 Meanwhile, heat a non stick frying pan until hot and spray
with the cooking spray. Brown the duck for 2 minutes on each
side over a high heat for duck that will still be slightly pink in
the centre, or cook for 3 minutes on each side if you prefer it
more cooked through.

3 Remove the pan from the hob and add the soy sauce,
honey, almonds and chilli. Turn the duck to coat in the sauce.

4 Stir the asparagus and make room for the duck. Nestle the
duck breasts among the asparagus and spoon the sauce all
over. Roast in the oven for 8 minutes and serve on warmed
plates.

Variation... Try making this recipe with two 125 g (4½ oz)
skinless boneless chicken breasts. Brown the chicken for
5 minutes on each side in step 2.

Chicken chilli fried rice

Serves 1
402 calories
Takes 30 minutes

60 g (2 oz) dried brown rice

calorie controlled cooking spray

125 g (4½ oz) skinless boneless chicken breast, diced

1 red pepper, de-seeded and diced

½ red or green chilli, de-seeded and diced

1 garlic clove, crushed

3 spring onions, sliced

juice of ½ a lime

2 heaped tablespoons chopped fresh coriander

This is ideal made with 150 g (5½ oz) leftover cold cooked rice as it's less likely to stick to the pan than freshly cooked rice.

1 Bring a pan of water to the boil, add the rice and cook according to the packet instructions until tender. Drain and rinse well in cold water.

2 Heat a non stick frying pan until hot and spray with the cooking spray. Add the chicken and stir-fry for 2 minutes over a high heat. Mix in the pepper and continue to cook for another 3 minutes.

3 Scatter in the chilli, garlic and spring onions. Stir-fry for 1 minute and then stir in the rice and the lime juice. Stir-fry for 2 minutes until the rice is thoroughly heated through. Mix in the coriander just before serving.

 Variation... For an easy vegetarian version, try the recipe on page 144.

Chicken, pesto and mozzarella parcels

Serves 2
235 calories per serving
Takes 25 minutes

calorie controlled cooking
   spray
2 x 150 g (5½ oz) skinless
   boneless chicken breasts
2 teaspoons sun-dried tomato
   pesto
60 g (2 oz) mozzarella light,
   sliced
salt and freshly ground black
   pepper

*The pesto and mozzarella stuffing adds plenty of flavour
and keeps the chicken moist and succulent. Serve with
fine green beans and 100 g (3½ oz) boiled new potatoes
per person.*

1 Preheat the oven to Gas Mark 6/200°C/fan oven 180°C.
Spray a small non stick roasting tin with the cooking spray.

2 Make a long slit along the length of each chicken breast and
open out to make a pocket. Spread the inside of each breast
with the pesto and then add the mozzarella. Close the chicken
breast and place in the roasting tin. Spray with the cooking
spray and season.

3 Cover the tin with foil and cook in the oven for 10 minutes.
Remove the foil and cook for another 8–10 minutes until
cooked through. Serve the chicken with any juices from the tin
spooned over the top.

Easy chicken and ham pots

Serves 2
405 calories per serving
Takes 35 minutes
❄ (pie filling only)

300 ml (10 fl oz) hot chicken
stock
300 g (10½ oz) skinless
boneless chicken breasts
125 g (4½ oz) broccoli florets,
cut into smaller florets and
stalks chopped finely
75 g (2¾ oz) ready-to-roll puff
pastry
1 tablespoon cornflour
50 g (1¾ oz) lean ham, diced
2 teaspoons dried thyme
2 tablespoons low fat soft
cheese with garlic and herbs
salt and freshly ground black
pepper

*These homely pies are simply delicious with green beans
and 50 g (1¾ oz) cooked new potatoes per person.*

1 Preheat the oven to Gas Mark 6/200°C/fan oven 180°C. Put
the chicken stock in a large lidded saucepan and bring to the
boil. Add the chicken and gently poach for 10 minutes until
cooked. Remove the chicken with a slotted spoon and leave to
cool on a board.

2 Add the broccoli to the same pan and bring back to a
simmer. Cook gently for 5 minutes until nearly tender.

3 Meanwhile, lay down a piece of non stick baking parchment
and roll the pastry on top of it into a rectangle until 3 mm
(⅛ inch) thick. Cut in half and put both halves on a non stick
baking tray. Bake in the oven for 10 minutes until golden and
risen.

4 While the pastry is in the oven, dissolve the cornflour in
2 tablespoons of cold water and stir into the pan with the
broccoli. Bring to the boil and simmer for 1 minute until
thickened. Cut the chicken into thin slices and add to the pan
along with the ham and thyme. Stir in the soft cheese until
combined and the chicken is piping hot and cooked through.
Season generously.

5 Spoon the chicken mixture into warmed bowls and top each
with a pastry lid. Serve immediately.

Fantastic fish and seafood

Thai prawn and pepper stir-fry

Serves 1

210 calories

Takes 10 minutes to prepare,
  15 minutes to cook

*This is a very quick and easy stir-fry using peeled prawns
and colourful vegetables. Serve with 60 g (2 oz) dried
noodles or long grain rice per person, cooked according to
the packet instructions.*

calorie controlled cooking
  spray

½ small red pepper, de-seeded
  and sliced thinly

1 shallot or ½ small onion,
  sliced thinly

1 large garlic clove, crushed

50 g (1¾ oz) mange tout or
  sugar snap peas

1 tablespoon light soy sauce

1 teaspoon dry sherry

¼ teaspoon sesame oil

a pinch of caster sugar

125 g (4½ oz) cooked peeled
  prawns, defrosted if frozen

a dash of hot pepper sauce
  (optional)

a pinch of sesame seeds, to
  garnish

1 Heat a wok or large non stick frying pan and spray with
the cooking spray. Add the pepper, shallot or onion, garlic
and 2 tablespoons of water. Stir-fry over a medium heat for
3 minutes, until the vegetables have softened.

2 Stir in the mange tout or sugar snap peas and cook for
another 2 minutes, until they have wilted.

3 In a cup, mix together the soy sauce, sherry, sesame oil and
sugar with 1 tablespoon of water. Add this to the pan, stirring
well.

4 Mix in the prawns and heat through until it is all piping hot.
Add the pepper sauce, if using, and serve sprinkled with the
sesame seeds.

Tip... Sesame oil is a brilliant addition to Chinese and Thai
dishes. It's very aromatic and adds lots of flavour. Don't fry
with it, however, as it burns very easily.

Variation... For an extra special treat, use shelled cooked
tiger prawns.

Baked haddock clementine

Serves 1

194 calories

Takes 10 minutes to prepare,
12 minutes to cook

150 g (5½ oz) skinless
haddock fillet

1 clementine, cut in half and
one half peeled and cut into
round slices, reserving the
other half for squeezing over

2 spring onions, sliced finely

1 cm (½ inch) fresh root
ginger, chopped finely

1 teaspoon soy sauce

1 teaspoon sesame oil

a few fresh coriander sprigs,
to garnish (optional)

*Serve this citrus flavoured fish with steamed vegetables,
such as carrot matchsticks and shredded cabbage.*

1 Preheat the oven to Gas Mark 6/200°C/fan oven 180°C.

2 Tear off a piece of non stick baking parchment about
30 cm (12 inches) long and fold in half to make a square. Place
the haddock in the middle.

3 Arrange the clementine slices over the fish and then sprinkle
over the spring onions and ginger. Squeeze the other half of
the clementine over the fish and drizzle over the soy sauce and
sesame oil.

4 Fold up the baking parchment, folding over at the top to seal,
and then tuck the ends under the fish.

5 Place on a baking tray and bake for 12 minutes until the
parcel is puffed up and golden. Open at the table to get the full
benefit of the delicious smells. Garnish with the coriander, if
using.

Variation... This can be made with a 150 g (5½ oz) salmon
fillet instead.

Fish 'n' chips for one

Serves 1
455 calories
Takes 40 minutes
❄️

175 g (6 oz) potatoes, peeled
and cut into thin sticks
1 tablespoon sunflower oil
½ teaspoon salt
175 g (6 oz) cod loin fillet
1 teaspoon plain white flour
1 egg white
25 g (1 oz) fresh white
breadcrumbs
calorie controlled cooking
spray
1 lemon wedge, to garnish

*When you fancy fish and chips, this recipe will guarantee
you satisfaction.*

1 Preheat the oven to Gas Mark 6/200°C/fan oven 180°C.

2 Rinse the potato sticks to remove the excess starch and
pat dry with kitchen towel. Place them in a plastic container
with a tight fitting lid, add the oil and sprinkle in the salt.
Place the lid on the container and shake thoroughly so all the
potatoes get a thin coating of salty oil.

3 Spread the chips out on a non stick baking tray and bake for
20–25 minutes, until they are golden and crispy.

4 Meanwhile, rinse the cod loin, pat dry with kitchen towel and
then dust it with the flour. Whisk the egg white until it becomes
foamy. Dip the fish into the egg white and then coat it in the
breadcrumbs. Lightly spray the crumbed fish with the cooking
spray and then place it on a non stick baking tray.

5 Bake the fish for 15–20 minutes, until it is cooked through
and the crumb coating is golden and crunchy.

6 Serve the fish and chips on a warmed serving plate and
garnish with a wedge of lemon.

Tip... Preheat the baking tray for 5 minutes before putting
the fish on to it, to make the fish crispy underneath.

Sauced sole with grapes

Serves 1
195 calories
Takes 10 minutes

10 g (⅓ oz) plain white flour
100 ml (3½ fl oz) skimmed
   milk
1 bay leaf
200 g (7 oz) lemon sole,
   skinned and filleted
a kettleful of boiling water
6 grapes
salt and freshly ground black
   pepper
1 lemon wedge, to serve
   (optional)

Although lemon sole has been used here, plaice works just as well. Serve with peas and 60 g (2 oz) dried rice, cooked according to the packet instructions.

1 Preheat the grill to high.

2 In a small saucepan, mix together the flour and milk. Bring to the boil, stirring. Add the bay leaf and cook over a very low heat for 5 minutes.

3 Grill the sole fillets for 3–4 minutes.

4 Meanwhile, pour boiling water over the grapes and then halve them. De-seed them if necessary.

5 Place the cooked sole and grapes on a serving plate, season the sauce, remove the bay leaf and pour the sauce over the fish. Serve with a lemon wedge, if using.

Spicy prawn open ravioli

Serves 2
202 calories per serving
Takes 20 minutes

calorie controlled cooking
    spray
4 spring onions, sliced
1 garlic clove, crushed
225 g (8 oz) tomatoes,
    chopped roughly
1 tablespoon fresh thyme
    leaves
4 tablespoons vegetable stock
1 teaspoon dried chilli flakes
1 tablespoon tomato purée
150 g (5½ oz) raw peeled tiger
    prawns, defrosted if frozen
110 g (4 oz) frozen peas
165 g (5¾ oz) fresh lasagne
    sheets (equivalent to
    4 sheets)
salt and freshly ground black
    pepper

*This looks superb and would be a great dish for a special
meal for two.*

1 Spray a large non stick saucepan with the cooking spray
and heat until sizzling. Add the spring onions and garlic. Cook
over a medium heat for 3 minutes until the spring onions have
wilted. Add the tomatoes and cook, stirring for 3 minutes until
the juices begin to run.

2 Add the thyme leaves, stock and chilli flakes to the pan. Bring
to the boil, reduce the heat and simmer for 5 minutes until
slightly thickened. Season.

3 Stir in the tomato purée, prawns and peas and cook for
3 minutes until the prawns have turned pink.

4 Meanwhile, bring a large pan of water to the boil, add the
lasagne sheets and cook for 2–3 minutes or according to the
packet instructions. Drain and rinse thoroughly.

5 Place a piece of pasta on each plate. Put a layer of the
prawn and tomato mixture on top, add another layer of pasta
and then top with the remaining prawn and tomato mixture.

Salmon en croûte

Serves 1

430 calories

Takes 20 minutes to prepare,
30 minutes to cook

**2 x 15 g (½ oz) sheets filo
pastry, measuring
30 x 40 cm (12 x 16 inches)**

**calorie controlled cooking
spray**

**125 g (4½ oz) skinless salmon
fillet**

**75 g (2¾ oz) frozen spinach,
defrosted and water
squeezed out**

a pinch of grated nutmeg

1 carrot, peeled and grated

**a few fresh mint sprigs,
chopped**

1 small garlic clove, crushed

½ teaspoon turmeric

½ teaspoon dried chilli flakes

a pinch of ground ginger

**salt and freshly ground black
pepper**

*Serve this delicious crispy parcel with a big mixed salad
and lemon wedges.*

1 Preheat the oven to Gas Mark 4/180°C/fan oven 160°C. Lay
the filo pastry on a work surface, one sheet on top of the other,
and spray with the cooking spray. Place the salmon in the
middle of one end of the stacked filo sheets and season.

2 Pile the spinach on the salmon, season again and scatter over
the nutmeg.

3 Mix all the remaining ingredients together in a bowl and
top the spinach with this mixture. Fold the pastry up at the
sides and over from the end. Keeping everything in place with
the pastry, roll the whole parcel over a few times until the
pastry is all used up.

4 Place the parcel on a baking tray lined with non stick
baking parchment. Spray with the cooking spray and then
bake for 30 minutes, or until golden brown and cooked right
through.

Spiced korma plaice

Serves 1
158 calories
Takes 15 minutes

175 g (6 oz) plaice fillet
1 tablespoon low fat natural yogurt
½ red chilli, de-seeded and sliced
1 tablespoon lime juice
½ teaspoon korma curry powder
a pinch of cumin seeds
calorie controlled cooking spray
salt and freshly ground black pepper
1 tablespoon chopped fresh coriander, to garnish

Deliciously spicy, serve with a tomato, cucumber and red onion salad.

1 Preheat the grill to medium high and line the grill pan with foil. Wash and pat dry the plaice fillet.

2 Mix together the yogurt, half the chilli, the lime juice, curry powder and cumin seeds in a small bowl. Season.

3 Spray the foil with the cooking spray. Put the plaice fillet skin side up on the foil and grill for 4 minutes. Turn the fish over and spoon on the spicy yogurt mixture until the fillet is covered. Return to the grill for 4 minutes or until cooked.

4 Serve sprinkled with the coriander and the remaining chilli.

Crab with courgette 'linguine'

Serves 2
100 calories
Takes 20 minutes

This fresh and vibrant dish will satisfy your tastebuds and your appetite. This works well hot or cold – as a starter or main course. Try using the courgette linguine instead of pasta in other pasta dishes too.

calorie controlled cooking spray

2 garlic cloves, crushed

1 red chilli, de-seeded and chopped finely

grated zest and juice of a lemon

400 g (14 oz) courgettes, sliced into ribbons

170 g can white crab meat, drained, or fresh white crab meat

a small bunch of fresh coriander or parsley, chopped

salt and freshly ground black pepper

1 Heat a large non stick frying pan and spray with the cooking spray. Fry the garlic for 1–2 minutes, until just golden.

2 Add the chilli, lemon zest and courgettes and stir-fry for 3–4 minutes, until just softened. Gently fold in the crab meat, lemon juice, fresh coriander or parsley and seasoning and serve.

Roast monkfish wrapped in bacon

Serves 2

494 calories per serving

Takes 20 minutes to prepare,
 30 minutes to cook

calorie controlled cooking
 spray

**600 g (1 lb 5 oz) potatoes,
 peeled and cut into 5 mm
 (¼ inch) slices**

2 x 225 g (8 oz) pieces
 monkfish tail, boned and
 membrane removed

grated zest and juice of ½ a
 lemon

1 tablespoon chopped fresh
 parsley

4 lean back bacon rashers

8 fresh sage leaves

1 onion, sliced

freshly ground black pepper

Perfect for a romantic meal for two. Serve with broccoli or fine green beans.

1 Preheat the oven to Gas Mark 6/200°C/fan oven 180°C and spray a large roasting tray with the cooking spray.

2 Bring a pan of water to the boil, add the potatoes and cook for 4–5 minutes, until just tender. Drain and spread them out on the roasting tray. Spray with the cooking spray and cook in the oven for 15 minutes.

3 Meanwhile, cut a pocket in each piece of monkfish and stuff with the lemon zest and parsley. Drizzle the lemon juice over the fish, season and then wrap each piece tightly in two rashers of bacon with the sage leaves tucked inside.

4 When the potatoes have cooked for 15 minutes, add the onion and turn the potato slices over using a fish slice. Sit the monkfish wraps in among the potatoes and spray with the cooking spray. Return the tray to the oven to cook for a further 15 minutes, or until the monkfish feels firm to the touch.

Variation... This recipe can also be prepared with other firm white fish fillets such as cod loin.

Seared tuna with Mexican salsa

Serves 2
260 calories per serving
Takes 15 minutes to prepare,
20 minutes to cook

**calorie controlled cooking
spray**
2 x 100 g (3½ oz) tuna steaks

For the salsa
½ red onion, diced
3 plum tomatoes, diced
**1 avocado, peeled, stoned and
diced**
**grated zest and juice of ½ a
lime**
a few drops of Tabasco sauce
freshly ground black pepper

*A simple but great tasting recipe – chunky fish with a spicy
salsa. Serve with steamed vegetables, such as mange tout
or baby corn.*

1 For the salsa, mix together the red onion, tomatoes and
avocado and then mix in the lime zest and juice. Add the
Tabasco sauce and season with black pepper. Cover and set
aside at room temperature.

2 Heat a non stick frying pan, spray with the cooking spray
and add the tuna. Cook for about 10 minutes on one side and
then turn over and cook for the same time on the other side.
Serve the tuna with the salsa.

Tip... Tuna is cooked when it changes from dark pink to a
light opaque pink – try not to overcook it as this will make
it tough.

Braised spicy prawns

Serves 1

92 calories

Takes 5 minutes to prepare,
8 minutes to cook

25 g (1 oz) mange tout

40 g (1½ oz) baby corn

**calorie controlled cooking
spray**

**60 g (2 oz) raw peeled prawns,
defrosted if frozen**

**½ green pepper, de-seeded
and sliced**

**½ teaspoon chopped fresh
root ginger**

1 garlic clove, crushed

**1 tablespoon yellow bean
sauce**

*This is a fantastic version of the vegetarian recipe on
page 130.*

1 Bring a pan of water to the boil and steam the mange tout
and baby corn for 6–8 minutes, until cooked but still crisp.

2 Meanwhile, heat a small frying pan and spray with the
cooking spray. Stir-fry the prawns, pepper, ginger and garlic for
4–5 minutes, until the prawns are pink and cooked through.

3 Add the yellow bean sauce and 3 tablespoons of water and
stir while it bubbles and thickens. Serve the prawns with the
steamed vegetables.

Blackened salmon on butternut squash

Serves 1

505 calories

Takes 30 minutes to prepare,
45 minutes to cook

**600 g (1 lb 5 oz) whole
butternut squash**

1 teaspoon ground cumin

**150 g (5½ oz) skinless salmon
fillet**

2 teaspoons soy sauce

**2 spring onions, sliced
diagonally into 2.5 cm
(1 inch) lengths**

**salt and freshly ground black
pepper**

To serve

a few fresh coriander sprigs

1 lime wedge

*This is an ideal recipe for a busy evening, as you can leave
the squash to cook in the oven while you get on with other
things.*

1 Preheat the oven to Gas Mark 7/220°C/fan oven 200°C
and bake the butternut squash, whole, on a baking tray for
45 minutes, or until soft when pierced with a knife. Peel,
de-seed and mash with seasoning.

2 Meanwhile, rub the cumin into the salmon and then brush
the soy sauce over the fillet.

3 When the butternut squash is nearly ready, preheat a non
stick griddle pan or the grill until very hot. Griddle or grill the
salmon for 3 minutes on one side without moving it, until
charred. Turn over with a fish slice and cook the other side for
2–3 minutes, until charred and the fish is just cooked through.
Griddle or grill the spring onions alongside for the last few
minutes.

4 Serve the salmon on a bed of the mashed butternut squash,
sprinkled with the coriander and with the lime wedge to
squeeze over.

Spicy crab cakes with sweet chilli dip

Serves 2

113 calories per serving

Takes 20 minutes +
   30 minutes chilling

❄ (crab cakes only)

For the crab cakes

175 g (6 oz) can white crab meat, drained

125 g (4½ oz) skinless coley fillet

1 large garlic clove, chopped

1 lemongrass stalk, chopped

1 medium-hot long red chilli, de-seeded and chopped

2.5 cm (1 inch) fresh root ginger, chopped finely

3 tablespoons chopped fresh coriander, plus extra to serve (optional)

1 egg white

calorie controlled cooking spray

salt and freshly ground black pepper

For the sweet chilli dip

3 tablespoons sweet chilli sauce

2 tablespoons 0% fat Greek yogurt

These make a delightful light meal or starter.

1 Put the crab meat, coley, garlic, lemongrass, chilli, ginger, coriander and egg white into a food processor. Season well and blend until the mixture forms a fairly smooth paste. Cover and chill for 30 minutes.

2 Meanwhile, mix together the sweet chilli sauce and yogurt to make the dip.

3 Shape the chilled crab mixture into six patties. Spray a large non stick frying pan with the cooking spray and fry the cakes over a medium heat for 3 minutes on each side until golden. Sprinkle with the extra coriander, if using, and serve with the sweet chilli dip.

Sardines with chermoula

Serves 2
192 calories per serving
Takes 18 minutes

½ red onion, chopped
1 garlic clove, chopped
4 fresh mint sprigs, leaves only
½ x 25 g packet fresh coriander leaves
½ teaspoon ground cumin
grated zest of a small lemon
4 x 50 g (1¾ oz) headless fresh sardines, cleaned
calorie controlled cooking spray
salt and freshly ground black pepper

Ask your fishmonger to remove the head and clean the sardines for you, or look out for headless cleaned sardines in the chiller cabinet. Serve with two slices of toasted low calorie bread per person and sliced tomatoes.

1 To make the chermoula, put the onion and garlic in a food processor and whizz until finely chopped. Add the mint, coriander, cumin, lemon zest and seasoning and whizz again until everything is finely chopped.

2 Preheat the grill to medium. Put the sardines on a foil-lined grill tray, spray with the cooking spray and cook for 6 minutes. Remove from the grill and turn over.

3 Fill the sardine cavities with a little of the chermoula mixture and place the remaining mixture around the sardines. Grill for a further 6 minutes until cooked and starting to char.

⊘ **Variation...** For a great tasting vegetarian version, see page 134.

Simply vegetarian

Veggie sausage and lentil conchiglie

Serves 1
246 calories
Takes 30 minutes

15 g (½ oz) dried Puy lentils
300 ml (10 fl oz) hot vegetable stock
1 garlic clove, sliced
1 fresh thyme sprig
50 g (1¾ oz) green beans, halved
40 g (1½ oz) dried conchiglie
2 vegetarian sausages

Puy lentils are a little more expensive than other types of lentils but have a lovely flavour and are well worth the extra cost.

1 Put the lentils in a lidded pan with the stock, garlic and thyme. Bring to the boil. Cover and simmer for 15 minutes until tender, adding the green beans for the last 5 minutes of cooking time.

2 Meanwhile, bring a large pan of water to the boil, add the pasta and cook according to the packet instructions.

3 Heat the grill to medium high and grill the sausages until browned and cooked through. Allow to cool slightly and then chop into large pieces.

4 Drain the pasta and stir into the lentils with the sausage pieces. Heat for 1–2 minutes until piping hot. Remove the sprig of thyme before serving.

Spanakopita

Serves 2

321 calories per serving

Takes 35 minutes to prepare, 25–30 minutes to cook

calorie controlled cooking spray

1 onion, sliced thinly

2 garlic cloves, crushed

300 g (10½ oz) spinach, washed

a kettleful of boiling water

50 g (1¾ oz) reduced fat feta cheese, cubed

1 egg, beaten

½ teaspoon caraway seeds

8 x 15 g (½ oz) sheets filo pastry, measuring 30 x 40 cm (12 x 16 inches)

salt and freshly ground black pepper

This Greek dish is equally good hot or cold.

1 Lightly spray a non stick frying pan with the cooking spray and heat until hot. Add the onion, reduce the heat and cook for 10 minutes until beginning to brown. Stir in the garlic and cook for a further 2 minutes. Remove from the heat.

2 Preheat the oven to Gas Mark 6/200°C/fan oven 180°C. Place the spinach in a colander and pour over boiling water. Drain, cool and squeeze out any excess liquid with the back of a wooden spoon before chopping roughly.

3 Mix the spinach and onions together with the feta cheese, egg and caraway seeds. Season.

4 Spray a sheet of filo pastry with the cooking spray and lay on a non stick baking tray. Spray another and lay it beside the first, but just overlapping, to make a square. Repeat with two more sheets, laying them the opposite way, but on top. Place the spinach mixture in the middle and spread to within 5 cm (2 inches) of the edge. Fold up the edges and then top with two more sheets of sprayed filo. Seal the edges. Repeat with two more sheets and then spray the whole thing before baking for 25–30 minutes until golden.

Pasta with baby vegetables and cheese

Serves 2
445 calories per serving
Takes 30 minutes

125 g (4½ oz) dried pasta
  bows
175 g (6 oz) baby leeks, sliced
100 g (3½ oz) petits pois
300 ml (10 fl oz) vegetable
  stock
15 g (½ oz) pine nut kernels
75 g (2¾ oz) feta cheese,
  crumbled
finely grated zest of ½ a lemon
salt and freshly ground black
  pepper

This dish is at its best served straight away as the heat of the pasta and vegetables will begin to melt the feta cheese, giving it a wonderfully creamy texture.

1 Bring a pan of water to the boil, add the pasta and cook for 8–10 minutes or according to the packet instructions. Drain well.

2 Meanwhile, in a small saucepan, cook the leeks and petits pois in the stock for 5 minutes. Drain well, reserving 3 tablespoons of the liquid.

3 Heat a small pan and add the pine nut kernels. Dry fry for 2–3 minutes until they begin to turn golden.

4 Mix the cooked pasta and vegetables together with the reserved cooking liquid, feta cheese, toasted pine nut kernels, lemon zest and seasoning.

Burrito with petit pois guacamole

Serves 1
468 calories
Takes 30 minutes

1 red pepper, halved and de-seeded

calorie controlled cooking spray

1 small red onion, chopped finely

1 garlic clove, crushed

150 g (5½ oz) mushrooms, halved

100 g (3½ oz) canned kidney beans, drained, rinsed and mashed slightly

juice of ½ a lemon

1 large soft flour tortilla

salt and freshly ground black pepper

For the guacamole

50 g (1¾ oz) petits pois

juice of ½ a lemon

½ tablespoon low fat natural yogurt

50 g (1¾) cherry tomatoes, chopped

½ shallot, chopped finely

15 g (½ oz) half fat mature Cheddar cheese, grated

This simple supper dish is very filling. Serve with watercress or a mixed leaf salad.

1 Preheat the grill to high. Grill the pepper, skin side up, until charred and blistered. Place in a plastic bag, twist the top and leave until cool enough to handle.

2 Meanwhile, bring a small pan of water to the boil, add the petit pois and cook for 3–4 minutes. Drain.

3 Heat a large non stick frying pan, spray with the cooking spray and then stir-fry the onion and garlic for 5 minutes, or until softened, adding a little water if necessary to prevent them from sticking.

4 Skin and chop the pepper. Add to the frying pan with the mushrooms, kidney beans, lemon juice and seasoning.

5 Spoon the bean mixture into the centre of the tortilla and fold over to make a parcel. Place in a flameproof baking dish.

6 Place the peas in a food processor with the lemon juice, yogurt and seasoning and blend to a purée, or mash with a fork. Fold in the tomatoes and shallot and spoon on top of the tortilla. Preheat the grill to high.

7 Sprinkle the grated cheese over the top of the tortilla and grill for 2–3 minutes, until the cheese is melted and golden.

Braised spicy beancurd

Serves 1

105 calories

Takes 5 minutes to prepare,
8 minutes to cook

25 g (1 oz) mange tout

40 g (1½ oz) baby corn

**calorie controlled cooking
spray**

60 g (2 oz) beancurd, cubed

**½ green pepper, de-seeded
and sliced**

**½ teaspoon chopped fresh
root ginger**

1 garlic clove, crushed

**1 tablespoon yellow bean
sauce**

A lively vegetarian dish with lots of flavour.

1 Bring a pan of water to the boil and steam the mange tout
and baby corn for 6–8 minutes, until cooked but still crisp.

2 Meanwhile, heat a small frying pan and spray with the
cooking spray. Stir-fry the beancurd, pepper, ginger and garlic
for 3–4 minutes, until the beancurd is golden.

3 Add the yellow bean sauce and 3 tablespoons of water and
stir while it bubbles and thickens. Serve the beancurd with the
steamed vegetables.

Variation... For a spicy seafood version, see the recipe on
page 114.

Quorn with pineapple noodles

Serves 2

379 calories per serving

Takes 15 minutes to prepare,
20 minutes to cook

100 g (3½ oz) dried rice noodles

a kettleful of boiling water

300 g (10½ oz) Quorn Fillets, defrosted

1 small can pineapple rings in natural juice, drained (keep the juice and chop all but two of the rings)

calorie controlled cooking spray

1 garlic clove, sliced finely

200 g (7 oz) Savoy cabbage, shredded finely

1 tablespoon soy sauce

½ teaspoon dried chilli flakes

This is a delightful vegetarian version of the recipe on page 60.

1 Place the rice noodles in a bowl and cover with boiling water. Leave to soak for 10 minutes or according to the packet instructions and then drain.

2 Preheat the grill to medium and place the Quorn Fillets side by side on the grill pan. Grill for 2–3 minutes until heated through.

3 Turn the fillets over and top each one with a pineapple ring and a teaspoon of pineapple juice. Grill for another 5 minutes, until the pineapple is golden around the edges.

4 Meanwhile, spray a large non stick frying pan or wok with the cooking spray and stir-fry the garlic for a few seconds. Add the cabbage, soy sauce, chilli flakes, pineapple pieces and juice.

5 With some scissors, cut the cooked rice noodles in half and then stir them into the stir-fried vegetables. Serve with the hot Quorn and pineapple.

Cheese and corn soufflé

Serves 2

321 calories per serving

Takes 10 minutes to prepare,
  1 hour to cook

**calorie controlled cooking
  spray**

2 eggs

25 g (1 oz) plain white flour

200 ml (7 fl oz) skimmed milk

**200 g (7 oz) canned
  sweetcorn, drained**

**60 g (2 oz) half fat Cheddar
  cheese, grated**

**½ green pepper, de-seeded
  and chopped**

**salt and freshly ground black
  pepper**

*Soufflés have a reputation for being tricky, but give this a
try and you will find out it's not as hard as you might think.*

1 Preheat the oven to Gas Mark 4/180°C/fan oven 160°C.
Spray a 700 ml (1¼ pint) soufflé dish (or 2 x 350 ml/12 fl oz
dishes) with the cooking spray.

2 Whisk the eggs with the flour and then gradually whisk in
the milk. Stir in the sweetcorn, cheese, green pepper and some
seasoning.

3 Pour into the soufflé dish or dishes and bake for 1 hour or
until puffed up and golden. (Individual soufflés will take around
45 minutes.)

Halloumi with chermoula

Serves 2
178 calories per serving
Takes 18 minutes

½ red onion, chopped
1 garlic clove, chopped
4 fresh mint sprigs, leaves
  only
½ x 25 g packet fresh
  coriander leaves
½ teaspoon ground cumin
grated zest of a small lemon
120 g (4½ oz) halloumi light
salt and freshly ground black
  pepper

This is a delicious, easy vegetarian version of the recipe on page 118.

1 To make the chermoula, put the onion and garlic in a food processor and whizz until finely chopped. Add the mint, coriander, cumin, lemon zest and seasoning and whizz again until everything is finely chopped.

2 Preheat the grill to medium. Spread the herb mixture all over the cheese and then grill for 3–4 minutes, until golden.

Marinated tofu and sesame noodles

Serves 1
390 calories per serving
Takes 10 minutes to prepare,
  10 minutes to cook

**100 g (3½ oz) firm tofu,
  drained and cubed**
1 tablespoon soy sauce
**1 cm (½ inch) fresh root
  ginger, grated finely**
1 garlic clove, crushed
40 g (1½ oz) dried egg noodles
**calorie controlled cooking
  spray**
**150 g (5½ oz) fresh or frozen
  spinach, chopped**
2 spring onions, chopped
1 teaspoon sesame oil
1 teaspoon sesame seeds

To garnish
**½ teaspoon dried chilli flakes
  (optional)**
**a handful of fresh coriander,
  chopped (optional)**

Marinating tofu before cooking gives it a great flavour.

1 Put the tofu in a small bowl with the soy sauce, ginger and garlic and gently toss together.

2 Bring a pan of water to the boil, add the noodles and cook until soft, or according to the packet instructions. Drain.

3 Spray a wok or large non stick frying pan with the cooking spray, add the spinach and spring onions and stir-fry for a few minutes or until tender.

4 Add the tofu and marinade to the pan and then add the noodles, sesame oil and sesame seeds. Fold gently together for a few minutes until the tofu is heated through. Serve garnished with the chilli flakes and coriander, if using.

Superquick spinach and cheese lasagne

Serves 2

686 calories per serving

Takes 5 minutes to prepare,
  20 minutes to cook

**calorie controlled cooking
  spray**

**200 g (7 oz) frozen spinach,
  defrosted and drained**

**100 g (3½ oz) low fat soft
  cheese with garlic and herbs**

**6 dried lasagne sheets
  (weighing 100 g/3½ oz)**

400 g can chopped tomatoes

**50 g (1¾ oz) half fat Cheddar
  cheese, grated**

**salt and freshly ground black
  pepper**

**a handful of fresh basil or
  parsley, chopped (optional)**

*There is no need to precook the filling for this vegetarian
lasagne, making it so fast to put together.*

1 Preheat the oven to Gas Mark 4/180°C/fan oven 160°C.
Spray a small ovenproof dish with the cooking spray.

2 In a bowl, mix the spinach and soft cheese together and
season with black pepper.

3 Place two sheets of lasagne in the ovenproof dish and
spoon over half of the spinach mixture. Place two more
sheets of lasagne on top and spoon the remaining spinach
mixture on to it. Repeat with the last two sheets, pour over
the chopped tomatoes, season generously and sprinkle with
the grated cheese.

4 Bake for 20 minutes or until golden and bubbling. Garnish
with the basil or parsley, if using.

Teriyaki mushrooms

Serves 1
341 calories
Takes 15 minutes

calorie controlled cooking
  spray
½ red onion, sliced
50 g (1¾ oz) sugar snap peas,
  halved lengthways
150 g (5½ oz) mushrooms,
  sliced
75 g (2¾ oz) baby corn
2 tablespoons teriyaki
  marinade
1 teaspoon cornflour
150 g packet straight-to-wok
  udon noodles

This is a filling and tasty version of the recipe on page 48.

1 Heat a non stick frying pan until hot and spray with the cooking spray. Add the onion to the pan and fry for 1 minute and then add the sugar snap peas, mushrooms and baby corn plus 1 tablespoon of water. Stir-fry for 2 minutes.

2 Mix the teriyaki marinade with the cornflour and 4 tablespoons of cold water, add to the frying pan and cook for 1 minute.

3 Mix the udon noodles into the sauce and vegetables. Cook for 1–2 minutes until heated through.

Florentine mushrooms

Serves 1
162 calories
Takes 10 minutes

**2 large flat mushrooms, stalks
removed**
**calorie controlled cooking
spray**
100 g (3½ oz) spinach, washed
**1 tablespoon low fat soft
cheese**
1 egg
**salt and freshly ground black
pepper**

A mouth-watering, vegetarian, cooked treat.

1 Preheat the grill to medium high.

2 Place the mushrooms in a flameproof baking dish, lightly spray with the cooking spray and season inside and out. Grill for 2 minutes, stalk side down, and then turn over and grill for 2 minutes more, or until tender.

3 Meanwhile, place the spinach in a lidded saucepan. Cover and cook over a low heat until wilted. Stir in the cream cheese and seasoning and keep warm.

4 Bring a separate pan of water to the boil for the poached egg. Reduce to a gentle simmer. Crack the egg into a small cup, stir the water creating a whirlpool effect and carefully add the egg to the water. Cook for 3–4 minutes, depending on how soft you like your egg yolk.

5 To serve, nestle the mushrooms side by side on a warm plate and spoon the creamy spinach on top. Lift the egg out of the pan using a slotted spoon and rest on top of the mushrooms. Serve immediately.

Tofu chilli fried rice

Serves 1
449 calories
Takes 30 minutes

60 g (2 oz) dried brown rice
calorie controlled cooking
   spray
1 red pepper, de-seeded and
   diced
75 g (2¾ oz) marinated tofu
   pieces
½ red or green chilli,
   de-seeded and diced
1 garlic clove, crushed
3 spring onions, sliced
juice of ½ a lime
2 heaped tablespoons
   chopped fresh coriander

This is a fantastic vegetarian version of the recipe on page 88.

1 Bring a pan of water to the boil, add the rice and cook according to the packet instructions until tender. Drain and rinse well in cold water.

2 Heat a non stick frying pan until hot and spray with the cooking spray. Add the pepper and stir-fry for 3 minutes over a high heat.

3 Scatter in the tofu, chilli, garlic and spring onions. Stir-fry for 1 minute and then stir in the rice and the lime juice. Stir-fry for 2 minutes until the rice is thoroughly heated through. Mix in the coriander just before serving.

Tip... If you like it hot, keep the seeds in the chilli.

Baked aubergine rounds

Serves 2

148 calories per serving

Takes 20 minutes to prepare,
15–20 minutes to cook

1 small aubergine, sliced into
12 rounds

40 g (1½ oz) dried polenta

1 teaspoon dried mixed herbs

1 garlic clove, crushed

1 egg, beaten

calorie controlled cooking
spray

salt and freshly ground black
pepper

mixed salad leaves, to serve

For the salsa

1 tomato on the vine,
de-seeded and diced

4 cm (1½ inches) cucumber,
diced

1 spring onion, sliced thinly

1 tablespoon chopped fresh
parsley

juice of ½ a lime

These crispy aubergine rounds are delicious.

1 Preheat the oven to Gas Mark 6/200°C/fan oven 180°C. Line a baking tray with non stick baking parchment. To make the salsa, combine all the ingredients and chill until ready to serve.

2 Heat a griddle or non stick frying pan until hot and cook the aubergine slices for 1–2 minutes, turning once, until beginning to char. Set aside. You may have to do this in batches.

3 Mix together the polenta, herbs, garlic and seasoning. Dip the aubergine slices first into the egg and then into the polenta, coating both sides. Place on the baking tray and spray with the cooking spray. Bake for 15–20 minutes until golden.

4 Serve the baked rounds on mixed salad leaves with a dollop of the salsa on the side.

Rich veggie stew

Serves 1

345 calories

Takes 45 minutes

calorie controlled cooking
  spray
1 small onion, chopped
1 garlic clove, crushed
100 g (3½ oz) Quorn Chicken
  Style Pieces
25 g (1 oz) ready-to-eat dried
  apricots, chopped
15 g (½ oz) sun-dried
  tomatoes, sliced
200 g (7 oz) canned chopped
  tomatoes
200 g (7 oz) floury potatoes,
  peeled and cut into chunks
salt and freshly ground black
  pepper

A dark, thick stew with a delicious tang of fruit and tomato.
Serve with steamed carrots.

1 Heat a non stick saucepan and spray with the cooking spray.
Fry the onion and garlic for about 4 minutes until softened,
adding a tablespoon of water if necessary to prevent them
from sticking.

2 Add the Quorn, apricots, sun-dried tomatoes, canned
tomatoes and 100 ml (3½ fl oz) of water and bring to the boil.
Turn down to a simmer and cook for 20 minutes, or until thick
and rich, stirring occasionally. Taste and season.

3 Meanwhile, bring a pan of water to the boil, add the potatoes
and cook for 15–20 minutes or until tender. Drain and serve
with the stew.

Delicious desserts

Fresh fig tart

Serves 1
199 calories
Takes 20 minutes

**calorie controlled cooking
  spray**
**40 g (1½ oz) ready-to-roll puff
  pastry**
1 fig, quartered
2 teaspoons clear honey
**finely grated zest and juice of
  ½ an orange**

*Fresh figs are at their best in September and October. Try
to find the freshest one that you can for this recipe.*

1 Preheat the oven to Gas Mark 7/220°C/fan oven 200°C.
Spray a non stick baking tray with the cooking spray.

2 Trim the edges of the pastry and cut out a 12 x 12 cm
(4½ x 4½ inch) square. The remaining pastry can be frozen.

3 Arrange the fig quarters on top of the pastry. Mix the honey
with the orange zest and juice and drizzle a teaspoon over the
tart, reserving the rest.

4 Bake on the baking tray for 12–15 minutes until the pastry
is puffed and golden. Serve warm with the reserved juice
spooned over.

Pear and cinnamon semolina

Serves 1

183 calories

Takes 15 minutes

15 g (½ oz) dried semolina
150 ml (5 fl oz) skimmed milk
¼ teaspoon cinnamon
1 teaspoon artificial sweetener
1 pear, cored and cut into wedges
calorie controlled cooking spray
2 teaspoons lemon juice

This is a far cry from the semolina associated with school dinners.

1 Place the semolina, milk and cinnamon in a small non stick pan and cook over a low heat for 3–5 minutes until thickened. Stir in the artificial sweetener and keep warm.

2 Heat a griddle pan or non stick frying pan until hot. Spray the pear wedges with the cooking spray and cook, turning once, in the hot pan for 2–3 minutes until slightly softened and striped.

3 Serve the pears on top of the semolina, drizzled with the lemon juice.

Luxury plum crumble

Serves 1

154 calories

Takes 10 minutes to prepare,
25 minutes to cook

2 plums, stoned and sliced

**1 tablespoon light muscovado
sugar**

2 teaspoons low fat spread

**2 tablespoons 'No Added
Sugar' muesli**

15 g (½ oz) marzipan, grated

To serve

**1 tablespoon 0% fat Greek
yogurt**

a pinch of cinnamon

*This muesli-based crumble topping is a far healthier
alternative to the usual buttery versions.*

1 Preheat the oven to Gas Mark 5/190°C/fan oven 170°C.

2 Put the plums in an individual ovenproof baking dish (a deep
ramekin is ideal) and scatter half the sugar over the top. Bake
for 10 minutes.

3 Meanwhile, prepare the topping. Melt the low fat spread
in a small saucepan or in the microwave, remove from the
heat and stir in the muesli, remaining sugar and marzipan.
Sprinkle the topping over the hot plums in an even layer.

4 Bake for a further 15 minutes, or until the topping is
crunchy and golden brown.

5 Serve with the yogurt, sprinkled with a little cinnamon.

Cherry meringue sundaes

Serves 2

345 calories per serving

Takes 5 minutes

400 g can cherries in syrup, drained

2 x 150 g tubs low fat black cherry yogurt

2 meringue nests, crumbled

2 tablespoons half fat crème fraîche

2 fresh cherries or 1 glacé cherry, halved, to decorate

A quick but delicious dessert that will satisfy sweet cravings. It is stunning when made in tall glasses, but you will need long sundae spoons.

1 In two tall sundae glasses or glass bowls, layer the cherries with the yogurt and crumbled meringue. Finish with a tablespoon of crème fraîche each and a cherry on top and serve immediately.

Variation... This is also good made with strawberries or raspberries.

Baked banana with passion fruit

Serves 1
188 calories
Takes 10 minutes

1 orange, peeled and sliced
1 banana, sliced thickly
1 passion fruit
1 tablespoon virtually fat free plain fromage frais

Passion fruit adds a wonderful exotic fragrance to this easy fruit parcel.

1 Preheat the oven to Gas Mark 6/200°C/fan oven 180°C.

2 Place a large square of foil on a baking tray. Sit the orange slices in the centre, add the banana and then scoop the seeds from the passion fruit and place on the banana.

3 Seal the parcel tightly, crimping and sealing the foil so that the juices can't escape. Bake for 7 minutes and then open up carefully and serve topped with the fromage frais.

Zabaglione

Serves 2

464 calories per serving

Takes 7 minutes

3 egg yolks

3 tablespoons golden caster sugar

3 tablespoons Marsala or sweet sherry

This warm and foaming mousse is very rich so a little goes a long way. Zabaglione is quick to make but needs to be made at the last minute.

1 Place the egg yolks and sugar in a heatproof medium size bowl over a pan of gently simmering water. Whisk together until they become thick and pale and have increased slightly in volume.

2 Add the Marsala or sherry and continue whisking until the mixture becomes warm and frothy.

3 Serve immediately in warmed glasses.

Variation... Marsala is a fortified sweet wine and is available in most supermarkets and wine shops. Try this recipe with dark rum or whisky if you prefer.

Peach brûlée

Serves 1

105 calories

Takes 5 minutes + cooling

1 ripe peach, halved and
   stoned, or 2 canned peach
   halves in natural juice,
   drained
2 tablespoons low fat natural
   yogurt
1 tablespoon golden
   granulated sugar or
   demerara sugar

*A very simple but tantalising pudding that you can make
for yourself in a just few minutes.*

1 Preheat the grill to high.

2 Place the peaches in a shallow flameproof bowl or plate
and spoon on the yogurt.

3 Sprinkle over the sugar and grill until the sugar is melted.
Cool for a minute or two until the sugar crisps up and then
serve.

Variation... Use virtually fat free plain fromage frais instead
of yogurt.

Easy chocolate soufflé

Serves 2
287 calories per serving
Takes 30 minutes

½ teaspoon low fat spread
25 g (1 oz) plain chocolate (minimum 70% cocoa solids), broken into pieces
1½ tablespoons Amaretto liqueur
2 eggs, separated
40 g (1½ oz) caster sugar
1 heaped teaspoon plain white flour
½ teaspoon icing sugar, to serve

If you avoid soufflés because timing the preparation and cooking is so difficult, you'll love these. Cook them in advance and when you're ready to eat dessert just pop them back into the oven – they fluff up beautifully.

1 Preheat the oven to Gas Mark 5/190°C/fan oven 170°C. Grease two 200 ml (7 fl oz) ramekins with the low fat spread.

2 In a small microwave proof bowl, melt the chocolate in the microwave by heating on high for a few seconds. (If you don't have a microwave, you can melt the chocolate in a small heatproof bowl placed over a saucepan of boiling water.) Briskly stir in the liqueur until you have a smooth consistency and then add the egg yolks, caster sugar and flour.

3 In a clean, grease-free bowl, whisk the egg whites until stiff peaks form. Fold the chocolate mixture into the egg whites with a metal spoon and divide between the prepared ramekins. Bake for 10–12 minutes until just starting to set and then remove from the oven and set aside to cool.

4 About 10 minutes before you want to serve the soufflés, preheat the oven to Gas Mark 6/200°C/fan oven 180°C. Pop the soufflés back into the oven and bake for a further 10 minutes until they puff up.

5 To serve, place the ramekins on two small plates and lightly dust with the icing sugar.

Variation... If you like you can use other spirits such as Tia Maria, rum or brandy instead of Amaretto.

Passion fruit cheesecakes

Serves 2
289 calories per serving
Takes 30 minutes + chilling

calorie controlled cooking
    spray
2 passion fruits
200 g (7 oz) low fat soft
    cheese
1 egg
1 egg white
2 teaspoons artificial
    sweetener
2 jumbo caramel rice cakes,
    crumbled

*This is a quick and easy way to make a cheesecake but it
looks very impressive.*

1 Preheat the oven to Gas Mark 6/200°C/fan oven 180°C. Line
the base of two 10 cm (4 inch) tins and spray lightly with the
cooking spray.

2 Halve one of the passion fruit, scoop out the flesh and beat
into the soft cheese with the whole egg and the egg white. Add
the sweetener and divide the mixture between the tins.

3 Sprinkle the crumbled rice cakes evenly over the top of
the cheese mixture. Bake for 20 minutes, but check after
5 minutes and cover the tops with foil if necessary to prevent
them from browning too much. Cool and then chill in the tins
before turning out on to serving plates.

4 Halve the remaining passion fruit and drizzle the ripe flesh
over the cheesecakes to serve.

Flaked rice pudding

Serves 1
198 calories
Takes 15 minutes

25 g (1 oz) dried flaked rice
1 tablespoon artificial
  sweetener
300 ml (10 fl oz) skimmed milk
a pinch of grated nutmeg

Rice pudding is always a favourite and perfect comfort food.

1 Put all the ingredients except the nutmeg into a small saucepan. Bring to a gentle simmer, stirring frequently and being very careful not to burn the milk.

2 Once simmering, reduce the heat to very low and continue cooking for 10–12 minutes or until thick and tender.

3 Transfer to a bowl and sprinkle with the nutmeg. Serve hot or cold.

Tip... You can also cook the rice in an ovenproof bowl in the oven at Gas Mark 2/150°C/fan oven 130°C for around 1½ hours.

Variation... If you prefer a dairy free version, you can substitute soya milk for the skimmed milk.

You can also omit the nutmeg and flavour this creamy dessert with fruit. Simply pour the cooked rice over fruit of your choice such as blackberries, sliced mango or banana.

Quick toffee apple pots

Serves 2
225 calories per serving
Takes 10 minutes

2 x 20 g (¾ oz) trifle sponges, cubed
2 teaspoons brandy
50 g (1¾ oz) dulce de leche caramel toffee
150 g (5½ oz) 0% fat Greek yogurt
½ apple, cored and cut into thin wedges
2 teaspoons demerara sugar

These super speedy puddings are just perfect for a winter evening. You will find the toffee sauce near the aisle with the ice cream cones and wafers in most large supermarkets.

1 Preheat the grill to hot. Take two 200 ml (7 fl oz) flameproof ramekins and divide the trifle sponges over each base. In a small bowl, mix together the brandy and 25 g (1 oz) of the dulce de leche. Divide this between the ramekins, drizzling it over the sponges.

2 In another small bowl, mix together the yogurt and remaining dulce de leche until smooth. Divide this between the ramekins, spooning it over the soaked sponges, and level the top.

3 Arrange the apple wedges over the top of each ramekin and sprinkle each with 1 teaspoon of the sugar. Put the ramekins under the grill and cook for 3–4 minutes until the sugar has caramelised. Serve immediately.

Variations... Try using other firm fruit such as pear. Use half a ripe dessert pear, peeled and cored instead of the apple.

If you don't want to use the brandy, replace it with 2 teaspoons of apple juice.

Roast pear and mango fool

Serves 2

207 calories per serving

Takes 10 minutes to prepare,
20 minutes to cook

2 ripe pears, peeled, cored and
each cut into 6 slices

1 orange, zest grated finely
and some reserved to
garnish, flesh juiced

1 large ripe mango, peeled,
stoned and chopped

150 g (5½ oz) low fat natural
yogurt

1 teaspoon artificial
sweetener, to taste

Pear and mango is a simply fantastic combination.

1 Preheat the oven to Gas Mark 4/180°C/fan oven 160°C and place the pear pieces in a small non stick roasting tin. Add the orange zest and juice and roast for 15 minutes or until the pears are soft.

2 Place the roasted pear and the mango pieces in a food processor or blender. Add the yogurt and whizz until smooth. Add artificial sweetener to taste, if required.

3 Tip into serving glasses or bowls and sprinkle with the reserved orange zest to garnish.

Egg custards with cherries

Serves 2

181 calories per serving

Takes 10 minutes to prepare +
20 minutes cooling,
25 minutes to bake

**40 g (1½ oz) dried sour
cherries**
300 ml (10 fl oz) skimmed milk
¼ teaspoon vanilla extract
15 g (½ oz) caster sugar
1 egg, beaten

*Dried sour cherries give these egg custards an unusual
twist – perfect for any occasion.*

1 Preheat the oven to Gas Mark 4/180°C/fan oven 160°C.
Put the cherries in a small saucepan with 5 tablespoons of
cold water, bring up to the boil and then simmer gently for
8–10 minutes, or until the liquid has just evaporated, ensuring
they don't boil dry. Share them between two ramekin dishes
or individual baking dishes.

2 Warm the milk in the same saucepan until just lukewarm.
Remove from the heat and add the vanilla extract and sugar,
stirring to dissolve.

3 Take care that the milk isn't too hot (otherwise the egg could
scramble) and then beat in the egg. Strain through a sieve into
the baking dishes.

4 Stand the dishes in a deep baking dish or roasting tin and
pour some warm water around them to come about one third
of the way up the sides. Bake for 25 minutes until set. Cool for
about 20 minutes before serving.

Tip... In step 4, standing the dishes in a baking dish with
warm water (called a bain marie) helps to create an even
temperature, which gives a smoother set to the custards.

Variation... Instead of dried cherries, use 75 g (2¾ oz) pitted
fresh cherries.

Strawberry tiramisu

Serves 2
187 calories per serving
Takes 20 minutes + chilling

8 **sponge fingers (40 g/1½ oz in total)**
4 **tablespoons orange juice**
150 **g (5½ oz) strawberries**
125 **g (4½ oz) virtually fat free plain fromage frais**
1½ **tablespoons caster sugar**

Serve these pretty layered desserts in elegant tall glasses for extra effect.

1 Break the sponge fingers into pieces and place half of them in the bottom of two glasses. Drizzle over a little of the orange juice.

2 Hull and chop the strawberries, reserving two for decoration. Place a spoonful on top of the sponge fingers in each glass.

3 Mix together the fromage frais and sugar. Spoon half the mixture on top of the strawberries, dividing it between the two glasses.

4 Add the remaining half of the sponge fingers, followed by the remaining strawberries and the fromage frais mixture to each of the two glasses.

5 Decorate with a whole strawberry and then chill for 20–60 minutes before serving.

Tip... If you prefer, use 125 g (4½ oz) flavoured yogurt – raspberry, strawberry or orange would work well – instead of the fromage frais and sugar.

Index

Other titles in the Weight Watchers Mini Series

ISBN 978-0-85720-932-0

ISBN 978-0-85720-935-1

ISBN 978-0-85720-934-4

ISBN 978-0-85720-938-2

ISBN 978-0-85720-931-3

ISBN 978-0-85720-937-5

ISBN 978-0-85720-936-8

ISBN 978-0-85720-933-7

ISBN 978-1-47111-084-9

ISBN 978-1-47111-089-4

ISBN 978-1-47111-091-7

ISBN 978-1-47111-087-0

ISBN 978-1-47111-090-0

ISBN 978-1-47111-085-6

ISBN 978-1-47111-088-7

ISBN 978-1-47111-086-3

For more details please visit www.simonandschuster.co.uk